MONEY FIGHT CLUB

BY ANNE CABORN & LINDSAY COOK

THE SMART WAY TO SAVE MONEY ONE PUNCH AT A TIME

Hh

HARRIMAN HOUSE LTD
3A Penns Road
Petersfield
Hampshire
GU32 2EW
GREAT BRITAIN

Tel: +44 (0)1730 233870
Email: enquiries@harriman-house.com
Website: www.harriman-house.com

First published in Great Britain in 2014
Copyright © Harriman House 2014

The right of Anne Caborn and Lindsay Cook to be identified as Authors has been asserted in accordance with the Copyright, Design and Patents Act 1988.

ISBN: 9780857193346

British Library Cataloguing in Publication Data
A CIP catalogue record for this book can be obtained from the British Library.

All rights reserved; no part of this publication may be reproduced, stored in a retrieval system, or transmitted in any form or by any means, electronic, mechanical, photocopying, recording, or otherwise without the prior written permission of the Publisher.

This book may not be lent, resold, hired out or otherwise disposed of by way of trade in any form of binding or cover other than that in which it is published without the prior written consent of the Publisher.

No responsibility for loss occasioned to any person or corporate body acting or refraining to act as a result of reading material in this book can be accepted by the Publisher or by the Authors.

Authors' photo by Simon Wicks

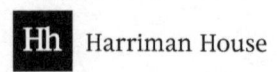

Hh Harriman House

For Emma, Gary and Rory who have been money fight club fighters since birth.

And Icon Design Partnership for the cover concept.

FREE EBOOK VERSION

As a buyer of the print book of *Money Fight Club* you can now download the eBook version free of charge to read on an eBook reader, your smartphone or your computer. Simply go to:

http://ebooks.harriman-house.com/moneyfightclub

or point your smartphone at the QRC below.

You can then register and download your free eBook.

FOLLOW US, LIKE US, EMAIL US

@HarrimanHouse
www.linkedin.com/company/harriman-house
www.facebook.com/harrimanhouse
contact@harriman-house.com

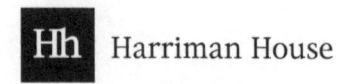

Hh Harriman House

CONTENTS

Why you need Money Fight Club	1
How the book is organised	5
Money management is a contact sport	7
Before you step into the ring	15
Why we're ripped off	19
What makes a money fighter?	25
The 6 Golden Rules of Money Fight Club	29
The Money Fight Club fitness test	31
Fighting styles	33
Your rights – adding extra punch	45
Why the good guy (or girl) wins	47
ROUND 1 – FOOD WARS	**49**
Price hunting	52
Food fighter tactics	55
Vouchers – double-edged swords	58
Cash-back cards	60
Never trust a till	60
Keep your receipts	61
Offers and unit pricing	61
Online food shopping	63
Food for thought?	65

ROUND 2 – HOUSEHOLD BILLS — 67
    Gas and electric — 70
    Council tax — 77
    Water — 81
    Phones — 84
    Television and broadband — 92
    Household insurance — 94
    Can you handle bills like a gazillionaire? — 96

ROUND 3 – BANKS AND FINANCE — 99
    Current accounts — 103
    Savings accounts — 108
    Debit, credit and store cards — 109
    Loans — 111
    Borrowing or saving – don't be grateful — 116

ROUND 4 – DEFENDING YOUR HOME — 117
    Buying and selling property — 120
    Renting — 138
    Home insurance — 143
    The word 'home' clouds our judgement — 144

ROUND 5 – TRAVEL — 147
    Travelling to work — 150
    Trains — 153
    Planes — 154
    Automobiles — 157
    Travel insurance — 169
    Don't think travel – think military logistics — 172

ROUND 6 – FINANCING THE FUTURE — 175
    When to start saving — 179
    Longer-term saving — 180

Pensions	182
Surprises around the corner	187
Meet your future self	194
ROUND 7 – TAX	**197**
The 2013-14 tax picture	201
Dodge the punches and land a few of your own	205
ROUND 8 – NEVER BE BLINDSIDED	**207**
Know what you have to spend	210
BEING PREPARED FOR THE WORST ISN'T ALL BAD	**217**
APPENDICES	**221**
Sample email	223
Sample letter	224
Directory	225
INDEX	**233**

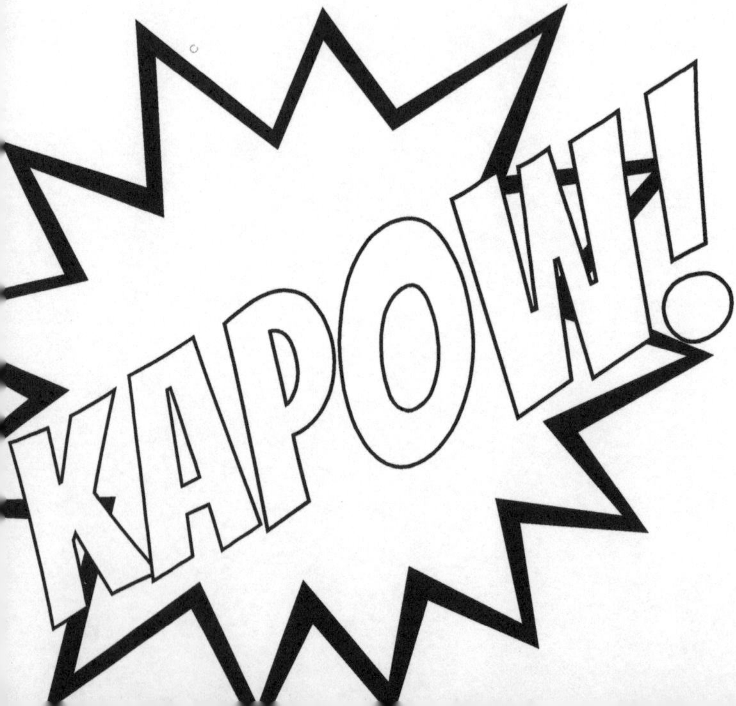
KAPOW!

WHY YOU NEED MONEY FIGHT CLUB

"I'm a fighter. I believe in the eye-for-an-eye business. I'm no cheek turner. I got no respect for a man who won't hit back. You kill my dog, you better hide your cat."

MUHAMMAD ALI

Whether it's dubious supermarket deals or failing banks, the modern high street is full of financial bullies who grab our cash and give us poor deals in return. You might think that with all the hoo-ha in recent years about a watchdog for *this* and a law to prevent *that* we might be safer, more protected. Wise up. Okay, so there have been huge technical advances to combat things like cyber fraud, and the internet means bad news spreads really fast so that cons and scandals are publicised more quickly, allowing more of us to avoid them.

But if anything, the 21st century presents us with an even greater likelihood of getting financially beaten up. You may be wearing boxing gloves and a gum shield, but you're facing ever more aggressive opponents with no qualms about fighting dirty and putting their profits, share prices and bonuses way ahead of looking after the interests of their customers. Plus, we're put in positions where we need to stand up for ourselves more often as we search for best buys, good deals and select from a growing array of financial products in an increasingly complex and crowded market place.

While we may have our guard up against obvious cons – such as emails from deposed potentates offering us huge sums in exchange for temporary use of our bank accounts – we assume well-known brands and high street names operate very differently. Forget that!

- Every single organisation with something to sell is after our hard-earned cash.
- An increasing number go to dubious lengths to get their hands on that cash.

It's not enough to defend yourself against their tricks and bullying tactics. You have to fight back. This book shows you how to avoid the scams and how to come out fighting if you don't get what you want.

- Bish! Spot and avoid the scams.
- Bash! Save money and negotiate better deals.
- Bosh! Win compensation or get your money back.

YOUR TRAINING PARTNERS

Anne Caborn and Lindsay Cook each have a financial black belt in money management and have floored more than one financial institution fighting for their own and other people's financial rights. They are the perfect training partners for your initiation into Money Fight Club.

Lindsay bought her first home when she was just 22, having worked out it was cheaper than paying rent, and has not looked back since. In the 1990s she became the first woman Business Editor of *The Times* and went on to become Group Managing Editor of Express Newspapers. She then set up as an independent consultant, helping turn around enterprises and bring spending under control for a range of companies in the UK and US. Lindsay also wrote the original *Money Diet* book in 1986. She is deputy chair of the Citizens Advice Bureau (CAB) in West Sussex.

Anne is a journalist and digital entrepreneur. She co-founded Make it and Mend it, an online sustainability website designed to help people make and mend more and throw away less, and she has worked in the National Health Service and the charity sector. In the 1980s she compiled the first British Rich List for *Money* magazine. This developed her lifelong fascination with the psychology of money and what divides those who are good with it from those who are not.

Lindsay and Anne both believe it's not enough to defend what you've got – you've got to go on the attack to combat poor deals and downright dishonesty, where world-renowned companies put their profits far above your best financial interests.

This book is Anne and Lindsay's training manual in unarmed financial combat. It will take you from raw recruit to Money Fight Club veteran in a few days, so you can cut your outgoings, spot what's dodgy and fight for fair treatment whoever you're dealing with. Plus, they'll direct you to an arsenal of resources so you understand your rights – and are ready to fight for them.

Money Fight Club is designed to change the way you think about (and use) money forever, and if you follow the combination of insights, advice, defensive manoeuvres and attack tactics presented here, you'll not only survive but win.

So, what are you waiting for? Release the financial fighter within yourself.

Welcome to *MONEY FIGHT CLUB*.

HOW THE BOOK IS ORGANISED

This book is divided into two parts. The first part is designed to toughen you up and starts out by giving you a little history lesson – how big business became so untrustworthy and all powerful, and how we all came to accept this state of affairs.

Once we've ripped off your rose-tinted glasses we'll slip on your boxing gloves and start to equip you with the fighting styles and defensive techniques you'll need, plus a quick financial fitness test designed to gauge your current strengths and weaknesses. You'll also find more help and advice on our website:
www.moneyfightclub.com

The second part of the book gives you the pointers you need to put these Money Fight Club techniques into action – whether you're battling household bills or buying anything from a new mobile phone to a pension. We'll highlight the scuzzy scams and dodgy deals. We'll show you how the marketing and advertising big business employs can trip you up. We'll also show you where to go for help and advice and how other money fighters have fought – and won.

This second part is divided into Rounds, one round for each of the main battle grounds:

- Round 1: Food Wars
- Round 2: Attacking Household Bills
- Round 3: Banks and Finance
- Round 4: Defending Your Home

- Round 5: Travel
- Round 6: Financing The Future
- Round 7: Tax
- Round 8: Never Be Blindsided

Each Round is further broken down into key areas, or pain points, so you can target specific opponents – supermarkets, banks and energy suppliers, for example. You can either work your way through the Rounds in order, or go straight to a specific area that you need to tackle as a personal priority, such as food bills (for example, why multi-buys can actually work out more expensive), or quick wins when it comes to getting your bills down, or when planning for the future.

And at the end of each Round there's a very brief section designed to get you thinking a little differently – more like a money fighter and less and less like a money pushover.

Now, let's get started.

MONEY MANAGEMENT IS A CONTACT SPORT

"People get much more bent out of shape about me being an ex-banker than they do about me being a convicted fraudster. 'You were a banker, oh my God.' Convicted fraudster was the first step of my rehabilitation."

GARY MULGREW OF NATWEST, MILLIONAIRE BRITISH BANKER WHO ENDED UP IN US JAIL, GUARDIAN

FIRST BLOOD

Open up your paper or turn on the news on any given day and somewhere between the latest celebrity indiscretion and the football scores you'll invariably find a financial scandal of one type or another. It will most likely involve a company you have a relationship with or, at the very least, one you have heard of. It will be to do with a brand name you recognise, a mainstream financial sector, such as banking, or an essential, such as heating or food.

It will involve smartly dressed, well-heeled people who've apparently engaged in a degree of monetary shenanigans that a cowboy builder might blush at – selling you a financial product you didn't need, billing you for a service you didn't ask for, charging you more than you actually needed to pay. It will have involved jargon and duplicity and a cavalier disregard for the basic rights of the consumer.

We only have ourselves to blame.

While we like to think we look after our hard-earned cash we're not in the habit of fighting to protect it. Our financial skills are based on a rose-tinted vision of an almost mythical financial past when

> **WHILE WE LIKE TO THINK WE LOOK AFTER OUR HARD-EARNED CASH WE'RE NOT IN THE HABIT OF FIGHTING TO PROTECT IT.**

the local bank was run by a man in the image of George Banks in *Mary Poppins* or Captain Mainwaring in *Dad's Army*, and who probably aspired to no more than the chance to retire to a cottage near Hastings. Forget them both. Instead, think Rambo.

Money management has always been a contact sport – and potentially a bloody one – so you need to get into peak condition and arm yourself accordingly. The reality is that anything to do with money (and profit) has always attracted its share of aggressive, cold-blooded, highly-skilled, well… Rambos. They're cold-hearted and calculating; merciless in their pursuit of financial victory.

In the past, most of us never came across them. If we had a pension it was provided by the state, or the company we worked for (possibly just one company for our entire working lives). We might buy our home with a mortgage but this was acquired from the building society where we'd saved our deposit. We might have some money in a savings account but it would be with the same building society, or with the bank we'd been with since childhood. We had our utilities supplied by companies that often had the word *British* in their names. The choice was whether you had a phone, not which of the myriad providers should bill you for it.

This situation was mirrored from the point of view of the Rambos. They moved through a financial stratosphere composed of well-advised, ultra-rich and corporate clients and they were unaware of, or at least unconcerned by, our existence. But they are aware now.

EXPANSION AND DEREGULATION

Things began to change in the years following the Second World War as aspirations amongst the working and emerging middle classes grew. Increasingly we were identified as 'consumers' and the word's meaning shifted in emphasis from what we used to how we purchased. Slowly but steadily, ordinary people had the ability and inclination to spend money in a way that the Rambos found interesting. We were moving into their world and they were moving into ours.

In spite of this shift, we were still pre-conditioned by a financial past that had insisted we leave key decisions in the hands of higher powers. Our parents (or, at least, their parents) put their faith in the National Health Service and the state's ability to provide (during sickness, unemployment and in retirement), in exchange for financial contributions deducted automatically from their pay packets.

Having been taught to trust our betters, we then fell victim to the old switcheroo. It wasn't just the state or our employer that would provide but a whole host of new and exciting organisations. Fast-forward and Margaret Thatcher allowed us to opt out of our company pensions and opt instead for private ones. We were offered choice and told it was a good thing. Not only were we looking at myriad products and services from a whole host of providers related to our health, wealth and lifestyle, but we were also seeking advice from a new industry of advisors and middle men whose own income came from the commission they earned on making a sale.

Money was on the move – state industries were privatised and new industries evolved that were eager to offer our hard-earned cash a range of new habitats. Rambos found new jungles where they could operate. The financial sector became more competitive (and less regulated), recruiting a new breed of employee to sell us a new brand of investments.

Home ownership was another area that underwent dramatic change. The range of financing options grew exponentially. You no longer needed a savings relationship with a traditional building society before you could borrow. Borrowing and loans with greater loan-to-value ratios (reducing how much of the underlying asset you were actually putting up the deposit for) became easier and at the same time the mortgage options became increasingly more complex. Lenders became plentiful. Why spend years trading up through increasingly better properties on which you owned more and more of the equity? Why not just buy big with a huge mortgage and rely on making a sizeable profit when you sell, to set it all right at some stage in the future?

Plastic cards increasingly replaced coins and notes and it became ever more acceptable to buy what you wanted on credit rather than saving until you had the money. For your great grandma 'buying on tick' was something never spoken about, but by the latter half of the 20th century how much you could borrow became as important a status symbol as what you actually had. A big house with a big mortgage was more impressive than a small house with no mortgage at all.

Easy access to credit also had the effect of speeding up decision-making. If you saved for a few years before you could afford that new home extension you had plenty of time to search for the right builder and decide exactly what you wanted done. Suddenly you could have the finance for a loft conversion in place in the time it took to watch a home makeover programme on television.

The late 20th century also encouraged us to go into business for ourselves; to take our own shot at becoming a millionaire. The emphasis was less and less on 'the state will provide' and more and more 'if you want it, go out and get it'. The more we aspired to, the more people were willing to offer us our dreams – but not necessarily to deliver on them.

AFTER THE REVOLUTION

The potential we offered to businesses selling an increasing range of things was breathtaking. What money we didn't have we could be encouraged to borrow in order to buy the things we didn't have. We could be talked into realising our dreams sooner rather than later and moving from one type of saving to another on future predictions (yes, just like crystal ball gazing) of what returns we might expect. We slipped on those rose-tinted glasses (again), while the people selling to us slipped on the boxing gloves.

So while financial scandals are nothing new – RBS, Northern Rock, Barings Bank, Enron, Banco Ambrosiano and all the way back to the South Sea Bubble disaster of the 1700s – the words 'money', 'investment' and 'fraud', or at least 'mismanagement' and 'misleading', found their way into the same headlines on an ever more regular basis.

Thanks to the financial revolution that had taken place, more and more of the money spirited away came from ordinary people who could ill afford to lose it. Even suppliers of life's basics – supermarkets and energy suppliers, for example – got in on the act by making it harder to understand what was on offer or how to identify the best option. We were sold the concept of competition but what we actually got was complexity.

Take the spring of 2013:

- March should have been distinctly chilly for payday lenders who were taken to task by the Office of Fair Trading (OFT) and told to get their house in order, but at the time of writing some months later we haven't noticed any change – except payday loan interest rates going up even more. The Financial Conduct Authority did propose tighter rules in October 2013 but money fighters know better than to wait for changes in regulation and legislation which can take time to bite.

- March was also the month that Which? launched a campaign to stop mobile phone companies raising phone tariffs for people on supposedly fixed-rate plans.

- April saw energy regulator Ofgem fine gas and electricity supplier SSE £10.5m for mis-selling, the largest fine it has ever imposed on an energy supplier.

- The latest round in the Libor interest rate fixing scandal saw Barclays duelling it out in the courts throughout 2013 with a company attempting to sue it. Meanwhile, in April of that year the Financial Conduct Authority (FCA) made Santander contact 270,000 mortgage customers about unclear information. A month later the FCA was back in the news, this time because it had uncovered as many as 1.3m borrowers who risked being unable to repay their interest-only mortgages.

- A day later British Gas was exposed for signing up customers to a fixed-price tariff that cost them up to £800 more than deals they could have got elsewhere. Oh, and oil companies were in the news over claims of price fixing.

- The spring of 2013 was also when the horse meat-in-convenience-food scandal hit. While the supermarkets would be the first to protest that they didn't set out to sell customers horse meat instead of beef, the scandal demonstrates how little trust we can place in the huge businesses we pay our money to.

These are just some of the highlights. If we wanted to list them all we'd need a bigger book!

The downside to all this apparent choice we have – from frozen lasagne to pension provision – is a highly competitive buying environment where companies rely on marketing and new offers to woo us and aren't really that concerned about whether we end up with fatty arteries and empty wallets some years down the line.

All this should be making you as mad as hell. Does it? If it does, what are you going to do about it – and how? Disappointingly, our financial skills are often not up to the task of responding in the most effective way.

We look for black and white but the Rambos give us 50 shades of very attractive and highly plausible grey. Modern marketing can actually make it harder for us to make sensible, informed choices – 'confusion marketing' is a recognised, if controversial, technique where the choices we are offered are so bamboozling that we cease to choose at all and simply go with the most hard-sold offer.

> **TODAY'S WORLD IS FINANCIALLY TOUGHER THAN ANY OF US EVER EXPECTED.**

These confusion techniques make it difficult, if not impossible, for us to decide between providers – new mobile phone anyone? – or compare prices. This is one of the reasons the UK government stepped in to try to force energy suppliers to simplify their tariffs.

The end result is that today's world is financially tougher than any of us ever expected or have been trained to deal with. We need to be fighting fit to survive. The good news is that Money Fight Club will show you how. If you look tough and talk tough you're less likely to be taken advantage of.

Don't just get mad – **GET EVEN**.

BIFF!

BEFORE YOU STEP INTO THE RING

"You can map out a fight plan or a life plan, but when the action starts, it may not go the way you planned, and you're down to your reflexes. That's where your roadwork shows. If you cheated on that in the dark of the morning, well, you're going to get found out now, under the bright lights."

SMOKIN' JOE FRAZIER

No fighter steps into the ring without doing some roadwork and research on their opponent. What's their killer punch? Do they feint right and follow with a left jab? Muhammad Ali floated like a butterfly and stung like a bee. So do businesses selling us goods and services.

As a member of Money Fight Club you must turn your back on your passive financial conditioning. One of the reasons why banks, supermarkets, utility companies and pension providers – to name but a few – have got away with so much for so long is because most of us keep quiet when things aren't going well. We often feel embarrassed to admit that an eye-catching promotion for a supermarket 'best buy' on washing detergent actually turned out to be much more expensive than the under-promoted budget brand on the bottom shelf, partway down the aisle (which we didn't initially spot).

People are conformists – we don't like to do anything that makes us look different from the rest of the tribe. If we spot something that looks amiss, most of us say nothing so as not to appear awkward or outspoken.

As our social status rests on our occupation, our car or our home, we do anything we can to preserve these outward symbols of status, even if at great personal cost. So if our personal finances look like a train wreck, we ignore the problem and brush it under the carpet (which we may have bought with a credit deal we didn't really understand when the carpet salesman sold it to us).

The good news is that even if just one or two people buck the conformist trend this exploitative system starts to break down. That's how revolutions start. That's why Money Fight Club members are important. Regularly standing up for our rights and screaming blue murder when we get duped can tip the balance and encourage everybody to fight harder to protect their cash. There are signs that this is beginning to happen.

MEET A FIGHTER...

Richard Herman from Middlesex got sick and tired of being cold-called by companies offering to represent him over an accident (he'd not had) or being mis-sold insurance (which he hadn't been). Despite registering with the Telephone Preference Service (TPS), he was still being pestered so he decided to fight back.

He tracked down the legal firms who were the ultimate clients of the companies doing the cold-calling and not only gave them a hard time but charged them for the time he was wasting on the phone. He thought £10 a minute seemed reasonable. In the end he took one company to court and received £195 plus £25 in court costs. Way to go!

Money Fight Club members are alert, focused, tenacious – and have a degree of cheek. They're not distracted by the marketing hype, they don't accept cold-calling as a fact of modern life and they certainly don't accept what big companies say about what we need to buy or how to make a claim.

Whether we're after a new sofa, a new gas supplier or financial redress, we decide what we want, what we're willing to pay, or how we're going to go about achieving this – without the help of the legal firm which benefits from the dubious cold-calling techniques.

We don't get dazzled by 'additional features', 'limited offers' or 'exclusive benefits' available with the latest version of this, that or the other. We know they're more likely to benefit the brands and retailers encouraging us to replace products, rather than us.

Money Fight Club members do our bit to remodel the consumer landscape by making it harder for rubbish companies to function. Without revenue coming in from consumers they can't survive, so we choose to purchase through those retailers and providers who make it easy for us to compare what they offer with the products of competitors, or choose between different offers.

Don't panic. We're not asking you to march into your local bank or mobile phone shop waving a big club and threatening to skin the manager. Yet.

Just stand up.

Right now.

And square your shoulders.

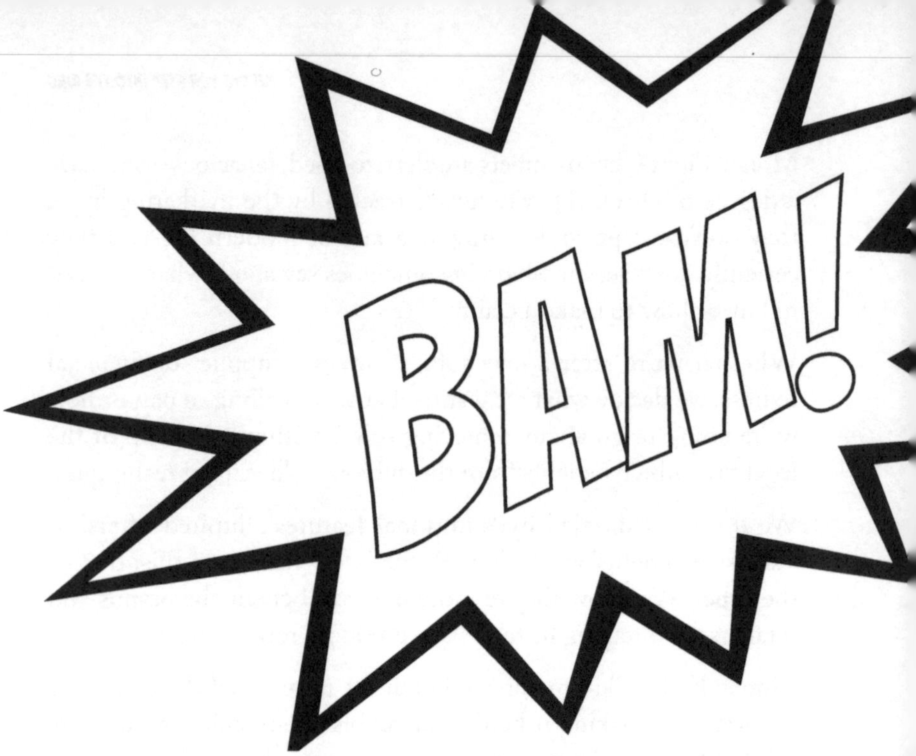
BAM!

WHY WE'RE RIPPED OFF

TOO LAZY, TOO NICE

Okay, sometimes we are blindsided by incompetent, greedy idiots in positions of power, but a lot of the time we should see it coming. There are two major reasons why we end up in positions where we can be ripped off in the first place:

1. We're ever so slightly lazy or, at the very least, not paying enough attention. Sorry, but it's true.
2. We're just too nice.

Let's face it, we sometimes don't look after the finances we have – never mind the new financial products we're considering. There are standing orders we forget why we're paying, or don't even notice, lost bank accounts and even piles of cash that reputable organisations are desperate to hand over to us.

In June 2013, the Treasury-backed National Savings & Investments organisation announced that it was sitting on 898,000 unclaimed Premium Bond prizes, worth over £44m in total. The smallest unclaimed prize was for £25 and the two largest were for £100,000 each. There will be good reasons why a proportion of these prizes haven't been claimed but in other cases the lucky owners have just forgotten, failed to update their address when they moved or haven't bothered to check up on old or lost bonds. Now that's just plain embarrassing. And a little shameful.

It's important not to fall at the first hurdle. Take this story about Lloyds Bank which surfaced in June 2013:

> The call centre which was handling claims made against the bank for mis-selling payment protection insurance was apparently telling its staff to reject claims out of hand, or use delaying tactics, on the basis that most claimants would just accept their claim wasn't valid or run out of steam when faced with delays. After the story broke, consumer organisations urged customers to resubmit claims, but how many people with a valid case walked away (and never went back) just because someone at a call centre told them they had no case?

There are reasons why we are too nice, or give people the benefit of any doubt too often. Society functions because we assume the people we deal with – even the ones we don't know – will do the right thing. Think about it. We'd never be able to drive round a roundabout or across a busy junction if we didn't assume our fellow motorists would give way, or stop at red lights when they're supposed to. Society only functions because we trust people and assume they're not out to do us harm.

The problem comes when we slip into nice (or, let's call it weak) patterns of behaviour in situations when we shouldn't. It doesn't help society function any better if we get ripped off when taking out a home loan or miss errors on our supermarket bill.

There are also other factors at play.

OPPORTUNISTIC SALES TECHNIQUES

Sometimes we don't sufficiently question the person offering us a financial product, even if we think they're glossing over less attractive features or putting a particularly rosy glow on benefits. We're too embarrassed, or we feel intimidated into silence. Most of us hate drawing attention to ourselves. It makes us feel awkward. That's why, at Money Fight Club, we've spent time watching how salespeople sell.

When you're accepting their offer a salesperson will often be looking down and getting on with the paperwork. Ask a tricky question and they give you their full attention – they may lead us to feel like we've interrupted the normal course of events or asked a silly question, as we're more likely to feel awkward if we think we've broken with normal codes of behaviour. With major purchases – financial or otherwise – we don't know what to expect so if we feel that we've breached financial etiquette it tends to put us on the back foot. That's one of the things that can make us reluctant to query total amounts even when they're more than we expect – oh, it didn't include the VAT then?

There's a sales technique when a deal is proving difficult to close, favoured in the home improvement sector. The customer is still unhappy about the price and the salesman reluctantly admits that there's one more discount they might be able to apply, but there doesn't seem to be any point. Why, asks the customer? "Because I still don't think you'll be able to afford it," responds the seller. It's amazing how many of us get suckered into indicating we jolly well could afford it at this stage. When the final price is revealed we can feel honour bound to take it. We're too embarrassed to say "no".

This is another reason why prices can be set unreasonably high at the outset but then reduce by 30%, even 50%. Sometimes the laziest way to bring an unwanted financial conversation to an end is to indicate you can't afford something. It requires less mental effort than arguing exactly what's wrong with the product and why it doesn't suit your needs. You say it's too expensive and bang, the salesman drops the price. You either have to admit that price wasn't the real problem (we're back to feeling awkward and embarrassed again) or accept the cheaper offer.

The thing to remember is embarrassment passes quickly. And who cares anyway as you're unlikely to see the person trying to sell you this particular something in the future; once a deal is closed you tend not to deal with the sales team again. Who cares if they still bear the scars of how you didn't buy or how you screwed every last discount out of them and were obviously prepared to walk away if you didn't like the price?

SOCIAL NORMS

Often we're won over by so-called free gifts and a very basic human response called 'the norm of reciprocity'. This means that if someone pays us a compliment or gives us something, we want to reciprocate. We want to believe the world is fair and that one good deed deserves another. Just think about how many financial products seem to offer you a free pen or other gift 'just for applying'. Would they really do that if it wasn't worth their while? Always look a gift horse in the mouth.

Our basic desire to believe good of other people is very creditable but we need to have our guard up when we're dealing with people we don't know. It doesn't matter if they're wearing expensive clothes and have a nice smile. It doesn't matter that they seem to know what they're talking about, are so very interested in our needs (particularly our financial needs), have a posh pen for us and ask after our children. Always take care. Always double-check EVERYTHING.

There are also less complimentary reasons why we get ripped off. One is that we can fall prey to flattery (there isn't a single bottle of expensive perfume or a luxury car that would ever be sold without a little of this). We are, after all, intelligent and discerning customers who deserve the best. We're sophisticated and absolutely understand all the facts that have just been rattled off at breakneck speed by the salesperson. If that doesn't work we might be treated to a sales patter about the rich and the famous who also drive this car or own this product.

> **ALWAYS LOOK A GIFT HORSE IN THE MOUTH.**

Or, even worse, we're the only person in our street that doesn't have one. This final one is called *social proof*. If you want to see how this works, stand in the street with a group of mates and look at the sky. The next person who comes along will also start looking skywards. This explains a whole host of dubious fashion trends! We don't like to miss out and we certainly don't like to stand out from the crowd. And, as mentioned earlier, we get embarrassed if we think we've contravened normal codes of behaviour.

TOO MUCH TRUST AND HOPE

Finally, it's just plain easier to trust people. Questioning and testing things takes far more effort. It can be positively exhausting.

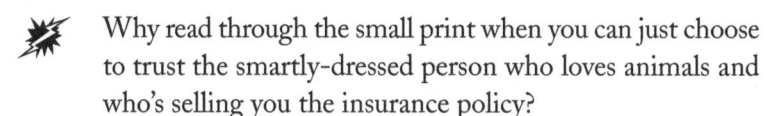

- Why read through the small print when you can just choose to trust the smartly-dressed person who loves animals and who's selling you the insurance policy?

- Why double-check our food bills when we can just assume the big supermarket we go to is on our side, has systems which are faultless and wants us to pay less?

- Why look at independent customer feedback websites when you can just believe what a company says about their product or service in very expensive ads and eye-catching literature?

- Why stand up when you can just back down?

It's easier to trust people than not to and we all suffer from a degree of financial inertia – apparently we're more likely to get divorced than change our bank account. Often we stick with things because they're OK, even if this means we're paying slightly more or losing out on the best interest rates. After all, you'll probably have to move again in a few months' time, right? We sweat to earn but we still make financial decisions like we have money to burn.

When it comes to making decisions about our future selves we can be tempted to hope for the best. For example, why put loads of money in a pension pot for the future when there are things you need (want) to spend your money on now. Retirement is such a long time away and what if you don't live long enough to enjoy it?

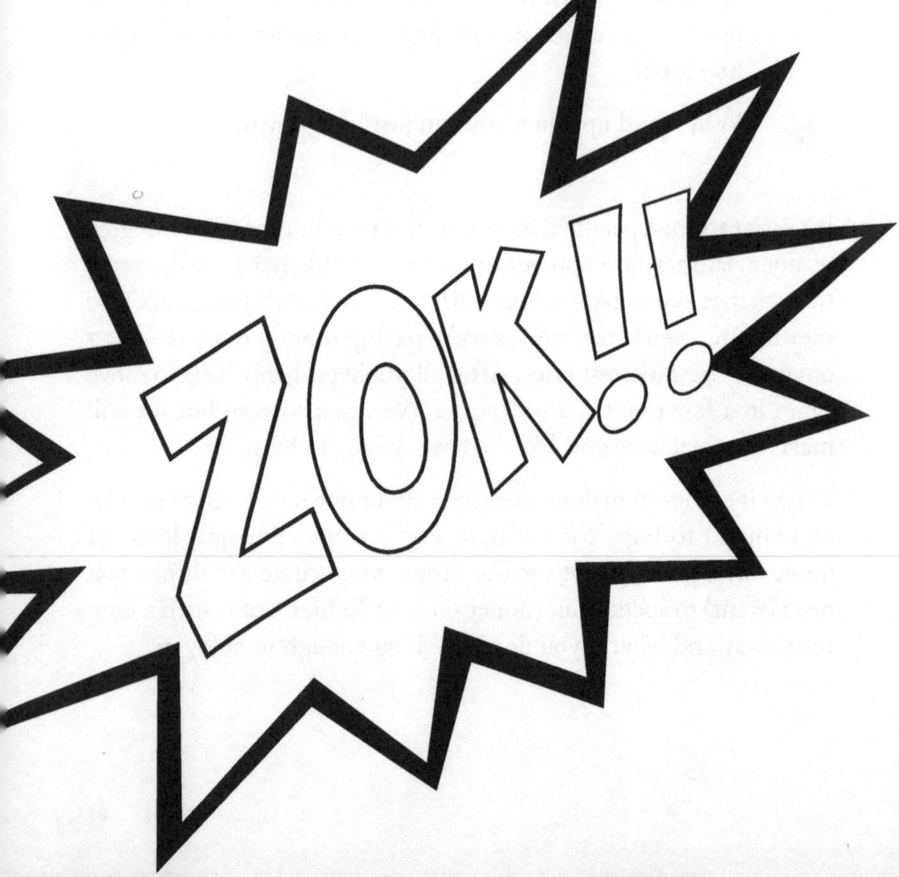
ZOK!!

WHAT MAKES A MONEY FIGHTER?

"In boxing you create a strategy to beat each new opponent, it's just like chess."

LENNOX LEWIS

If you were a boxer or a cage fighter you'd be a winner if you were faster on your feet than your opponent and had the right moves. You'd win if you packed a big enough punch. We can show you how to do that. But you also need to hone your instincts:

- **Be wary** – it's ok to trust people we know well but don't trust a stranger just because he wears a suit or works in a bank. If something doesn't sound right, investigate. Ask questions. Look for evidence.

- **Don't be distracted** – friendly chat about family, jokey banter, flattery and free gifts when buying financial products all encourage us to let our guard down.

- **Stay calm when under attack** – big budget adverts, big posters at the bus stop, celebrity endorsements and in-store, on-pack promotions promising us discounts, or so much extra for free, can get us way too excited. Keep a level head. Ignore the promotion and do the mental arithmetic before you buy.

- **Be prepared to tough it out** – sometimes getting what you want can be exhausting. You may have to ask loads of questions, or be prepared to mount a counter argument while people try to dismiss your claim. If you snooze you lose.

- **Seek allies** – if you feel out of your depth get a good coach, as well as this book. That could mean using online price comparison sites or taking along a friend who'll stand in your corner (and act as a witness to what's said) at a face-to-face meeting. It could mean making your views known on customer review sites or through social media groups on Twitter or Facebook. But don't get suckered in by cold calls from claims advice companies or 'no win-no fee' legal firms who want to act on your behalf.

- **Take your time** – it's better to miss a deal than snap it up and regret it. The next 'bargain' is just around the corner. And when it comes to fighting for your rights you're more likely to win on points than with a knock out. It may take several letters and threatening to take someone to court – not just one angry phone call. Even big businesses can run out of stamina if you put them under relentless attack.

- **Stay in control** – if you want to buy something, do your research; don't just go with the next salesman who rings you up, or the next flyer that lands on your doormat. Before talking to anyone you need to work out what you want, when you want it and the price you want to pay.

BE STRONGER AND TOUGHER

To not only survive but thrive we need to be stronger and tougher than we're naturally inclined to be. You need to chase the best deals and be prepared to move providers to get them. You draw attention to the problem; you phone, you email and write – you fight. You take the battle to customer service desks, overseas call centres, head offices and, if necessary, the courts.

From a pension shortfall due to poor fund performance and excessive charges, or a few pounds extra at the supermarket because an offer wasn't deducted at the till, be prepared to come out fighting.

It may be as simple as complaining loudly (but politely) to the branch manager. It might mean writing letters to an organisation and threatening to take your case against a large financial organisation to their ombudsman. You don't back down because it looks too hard or too time-consuming.

Like all fighters you train hard and come prepared:

- Sharpen up your phone, letter writing and email skills to get your point across quickly and clearly.
- Do your research and always send letters to named individuals (and an extra copy to the most senior person you can find in that organisation).
- Check your rights and what the law has to say on the subject.

As a Money Fight Club member you're quite prepared to square up to Chief Executives and Directors. Show no fear. You've done the roadwork. And remember, this book is in your corner.

❝ BE PREPARED TO COME OUT FIGHTING. ❞

Now, even cage fighting has some rules...

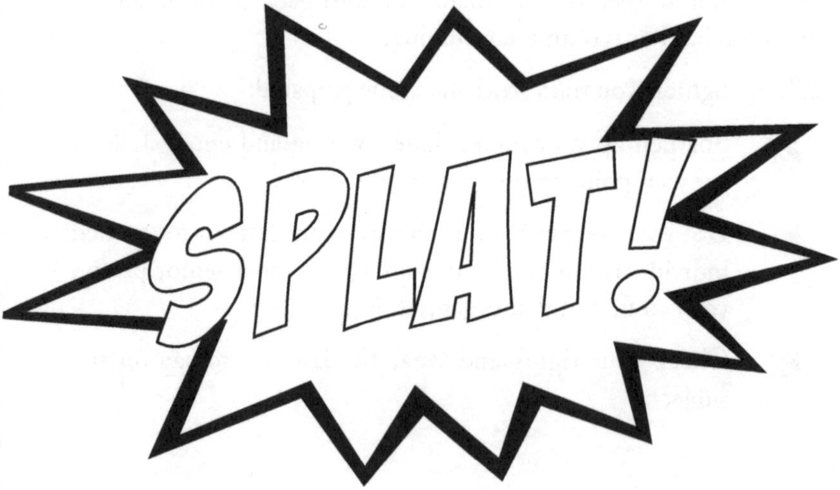
SPLAT!

THE 6 GOLDEN RULES OF MONEY FIGHT CLUB

1. The first rule of Money Fight Club is **TALK ABOUT MONEY FIGHT CLUB**. In the playground, in the office, at the gym and over the dinner table. Share tips and warnings about cons you've uncovered. Forget telling people what car you drive – tell them how you made a business behemoth back down and quiver a little.

2. **Arm yourself.** Money Fight Club members know their rights, what the law says and which authorities to complain to if they don't get what they demand. Don't worry. We'll equip you with knowledge of your rights and techniques for using them.

3. **Be heard.** It doesn't matter whether you're talking to the supermarket manager about your food bill or the bank manager about your mortgage, your voice is clear and confident. Sometimes you're more likely to get what you want if other customers hear you complain (calmly but with ice in your voice).

4. **Never lose your temper.** Money Fight Club members keep a cool head. Uncontrolled anger and abusive language just give the big brands and financial bullies an excuse not to listen to you.

5. **Pay attention to detail**. Not only are you prepared to write articulate emails and letters, but you take time to check the names, titles and addresses of the people you need to contact and what rights you're choosing to exercise. Check basics, such as spellings, before you send anything in writing.

6. **Don't give up**. Okay, there may be times when you have to walk away, but never give up without a fight! Then get ready for the next one because – trust us – it's just around the corner.

THE MONEY FIGHT CLUB FITNESS TEST

As with any development process it's useful to know where you are right now – do you need to drop a few pounds (figuratively speaking) and how good is your stamina, for example?

There's a more extensive Money Fight Club fitness test on our website (**www.moneyfightclub.com**) but the one below will give you a rough idea of how you currently shape up.

Everybody's different so some combat techniques may already be part of your fighting style. Try this simple test and see.

Answer 'Never', 'Sometimes' or 'Always' to the statements below:

- You check till receipts and get mistakes corrected.
- You take time to read any small print before you sign something.
- You ask questions and more questions until you understand something completely.
- If you believe you're in the right you'll fight until you get what you deserve.
- You assume that the person selling you something does not automatically put your best interests first.
- You believe that if something sounds too good to be true it is too good to be true.

How did you do?

Count up how many times you said 'Never', 'Sometimes' or 'Always'.

- **More 'Always' responses**: You already understand a lot of the Fight Club basics and probably carry a few battle scars to prove it, but now's the time to raise your game. It's not just fighting your corner more often, but also taking on bigger and bigger opponents. It's also important that you think through each decision on its merits and don't just say "no" out of habit. Turning everything down is just as lazy as saying "yes" to everything.

- **More 'Sometimes' responses**: You will check things and are aware that you can't automatically trust shops or financial institutions to get things right. Chances are the recent headlines around financial selling and retail scams have put you on your metal. But there's still more you can do. You may need to improve your research or attention to detail. It may be that you get a little battle weary sometimes. If that's the case, choose your battles carefully and focus on the ones where there's more at stake.

- **More 'Never' responses**: You have a tendency to accept things at first glance and assume they're right. This could be because you're so busy it's hard to find the time to go through the detail. You need to prioritise – some things are worth fighting over more than others. Allocate enough time to make big financial decisions (and some of the regular small ones, such as checking shop receipts for errors) and don't be afraid to go back and query something later. It's your money and you've worked hard for it. Defend it! Keep a tally of how much you're saving and see how it mounts up over the weeks and months.

FIGHTING STYLES

Depending on the financial terrain and who you're pitting your skills against, you may need to adopt different techniques. Money Fight Club members are skilled in all of them.

FACE-TO-FACE COMBAT

This is the essential fighting style for those initial skirmishes in shops, supermarkets, at the bank counter, or down the garage.

The first rule of face-to-face combat is – stay calm. If you get angry, chances are the person you're talking to will get angry too, or call security, or refuse to speak to you any further (including call centre operatives, who will drop your call).

The key thing is to keep the dialogue going. Rude words and a red face just weaken your case. And don't waste time. Be focused on what you want to happen – a refund, a replacement, an apology. Dominate the arena – whether it's the supermarket or the bank.

THE POLITENESS GAMBIT

If a shop assistant has been standing on their feet in a busy high street store and the next thing somebody's bending their ear with a complaint, they may just go on the defensive. Try the politeness gambit first. There's no harm in acknowledging how busy they are and making it clear your complaint isn't personally to do with them (unless it is).

But don't be apologetic. A bad opening line is: "I'm sorry to bother you." You have nothing to be sorry about. You can start with: "I can see you're busy but this is really important and can't wait. It's a serious complaint – not against you. Do you want to call your boss to deal with it?"

DON'T TELL THEM HOW YOU'RE FEELING - TELL THEM WHAT YOU WANT

Often we feel so frustrated when we're overcharged or mis-sold to that we want the person or business responsible to just start out by acknowledging this. The problem is that this all takes time. You're a fighter, so you don't acknowledge your wounds in public. Tell them what you want them to do, not how you feel:

- "I've noticed I've been overcharged and I need the money refunded to my card please."
- "The policy you sold me isn't right for my needs as I explained them to you and I need you to rectify this."
- "I plan to make a formal complaint about this and I need you to supply details of your internal complaints procedure."

BE AUDIBLE

It's amazing how often people who are complaining lower their voices. As we've said already, you've got nothing to be apologetic or ashamed about. A clear, audible voice, which may well be overheard by other customers, is a good first attack, as long as you're clear and calm. Never shout. Never swear. Just be heard.

If the person you're speaking with is wearing a name badge use their name in the conversation and let them feel they have some positive control. "I'm sorry Fred, but that's not what I need to happen. What else can you offer me? Do you need me to talk to your boss about this? I don't want to pressure you into exceeding your personal authority."

BE PREPARED TO PUNCH ABOVE YOUR WEIGHT

If the person you're dealing with can't help, ask to see their boss. If their boss isn't there get the boss's name and a time when they will be in, or get their work phone number if they are in another office. Then follow through. Your heart may be pounding but they don't know that. Be patient but be persistent. If you ask them to do something and they say they can't do it, don't just ask why; find out what they *can* do for you. "Well if you can't give me your boss's direct line how can *you* help me with this problem?"

BODY LANGUAGE

Our body language can have a profound influence on how people interact with us. Do you look small and apologetic or tall and confident? Remember that your body language also affects the way you present yourself in any medium, so adopting a relaxed but authoritative stance can influence the way we sound on the phone; even the way we approach writing an email or letter. Our body language can influence how we *feel* too. Adopt a powerful stance and you feel more powerful. Adopt a relaxed stance and you feel less stressed.

Approach any complaint with your posture erect (even when sitting) and with your hands relaxed, not clenched. Adjust your body until you feel comfortable and in charge. In a face-to-face meeting look whoever you're talking to in the eye but don't lock them into a stare. Likewise, don't face them squarely but at a slight angle. Square on and too close can come across as very aggressive and put people on the defensive.

If things are not going well you can move into more of a head-to-head pose and harden your features, so they can see you're not being moved (look resolute rather than just angry or aggressive). If they are responding positively, soften your features or even smile and nod to show they're getting somewhere. But keep your guard up.

BEND THEIR EAR BY PHONE

The great thing about a phone conversation is you can write notes and reminders in advance and have them in front of you while you're speaking. Make sure you have all the details you need, such as the date of the transaction, or the policy number.

Get comfy in your chair, with all the papers you need laid out in front of you. Ideally, make the call from a room with no distractions and where you're unlikely to be disturbed. Making these calls from work isn't a good idea.

It's worth spending time checking out who you could or should complain to next – such as the ombudsman for that service, or the professional association that regulates that business. Drop these details into the conversation.

Check the numbers you plan to use before you pick up the phone. Some organisations publicise premium rate numbers but you need to hunt around for the less expensive numbers to call. Research carried out by phone regulator Ofcom published in May 2013 discovered that some people put off making important calls because they're worried about the charges they may incur.

Ofcom wants to simplify how we are charged for different types of numbers and the different charges we face when we call from a mobile rather than a landline but in the meantime don't be afraid to ask an organisation to call you back.

If you do have to use a premium rate phone number it's even more important that you write down the points you want to get across and that you're clear and unequivocal when you speak, so you don't have to waste time (and money) repeating yourself.

GET TO KNOW YOUR OPPONENT

Sometimes calls will start with the person on the other end of the line introducing themselves. Make a note of their name and use it. It helps to establish a dialogue.

Keep in mind that many call centres are working to pre-written scripts, which they have to follow, so be clear and succinct:

- "I'm ringing to make a complaint about something you sold me."
- "I need a faulty item replaced."
- "I want details of your internal complaints procedure."

Talk in short, concise sentences. Don't rush what you have to say. If dealing with a call centre abroad, consider that someone may be speaking to you in their second language – you need them to understand you.

Sound cool or icy cold – depending on how the call goes. Warm up your voice if you start to get what you want. How you look is how you sound. If you have a smile on your face this comes across in your voice – even if people can't see you. If you're squaring up to make a complaint on the phone, set your jaw and be tight-lipped.

Practice deepening your voice a little before you begin the call. Take a deep full breath before you start to speak.

Whoever you speak to, always try to get their name, job title and a direct phone number before you end the call. Don't rely on some unnamed individual phoning you back even if they promise to do so. Some organisations will give a complaint a reference number. Keep a note of that as well, along with the date and time of your call. It will make pursuing matters further much easier.

If you build a relationship with the person on the other end of the phone, find out if they are willing to follow through with your case and get their full name and direct line.

BE READY TO STRIKE ABOVE THE HEAD

As with face-to-face combat, don't waste time. Make sure you have all the details clear in your head or in notes in front of you. Your time is important, particularly if you're paying for the call, and the call centre worker will also be trying to get you off the phone and on to the next call, so if you do not have the information to hand you may have to call back.

If the call isn't progressing, ask to speak to a supervisor. At this stage make it clear to the person you are speaking to that you aren't going to complain about them (unless you are), but that it's becoming obvious that you need to speak to someone more senior. Not all call centres will allow you to do this, but it is worth asking.

Don't regard getting through to a supervisor as a victory by itself. They may take your call reluctantly and not have much more authority, particularly if the call centre is working for loads of different companies rather than one particular business or brand. What is your gut telling you? Is the supervisor able to make decisions and cut deals? If not move on to a different method – you could try to get a work phone number for a member of the company's senior management, or write to its head office.

If someone has been polite and tried to help acknowledge that. If you get shirty it's always possible the call might be disconnected. Companies have a right to protect their staff from abusive or aggressive customers and calls can be terminated in these circumstances.

STAY ALERT

Make notes of what's being said to you. Ask people to repeat things or to speak more slowly, so they know you're writing things down. You can also ask them to follow up by email or in writing.

Make it clear that if their response is unsatisfactory you have every intention of taking things further. If you intend to follow up by email or letter, or have asked them to do so with you, always get names and contact details before you end the call.

GET YOUR AIM RIGHT WITH EMAIL

Email is so wonderfully easy but when it comes to fighting your financial corner it can be a bit like shooting in the dark. Don't rely on sending emails to addresses of the form 'customerservice@...' or 'info@...'.

By all means use an address like that but also look for named individuals to send to by checking out the organisation's website thoroughly and searching on the internet. Sometimes you can find useful names and email addresses by checking news releases or press information published by the organisation or elsewhere on the web.

Sometimes just typing the right words into a search engine can yield results, such as 'head of customer service [name of firm]' or even 'director [name of firm]'. Also try business websites such as LinkedIn. On business networking sites you can search for people by the organisation they work for.

If you have someone's name but not their email address you can sometimes work this out for yourself. If other email addresses for people in that organisation are of the form 'firstname.surname@...' the chances are theirs will be too.

When you fire off that email make sure you have at least two named individuals in your sights – the main person you want to target and their boss is a good combination. The old one-two.

You can find a sample email to follow at the back of this book. You can also find a downloadable version on our website **www.moneyfightclub.com**.

THE SWEET SCIENCE OF GETTING YOUR POINT ACROSS BY LETTER

Letter writing can be seen as a little old school but it packs a punch. Boxing was traditionally called the "sweet science" because it was considered more gentlemanly than fighting with swords or shooting. You can still give someone a bloody nose or a black eye with a well-aimed letter.

You can use the same seek-and-destroy tactics mentioned in the email section above to find the names and addresses of the individuals you need to target. Here's a quick guide to how your letter should shape up:

Your letter needs to go to the chief executive's office, addressed by name and with the correct postal address. It should state what the problem is, what measures you have taken to resolve the issue and most importantly what you want the CEO to do. Lastly, you need to make it clear you know which regulator or ombudsman would deal with the issue if the company will not do what you want.

You can find a template letter at the back of this book. You can also find downloadable versions on our website:
www.moneyfightclub.com

MEET A FIGHTER...

Nigel Cox bought a computer online from Acer but had some problems with it once it had arrived. Acer tested the computer but couldn't find a fault. They did offer a refund but wanted to deduct a collection fee and a further amount for damage it claimed had been caused by Nigel.

Nigel combatted this using distance selling regulations designed to cover you when you buy online – see our legislation section in the directory at the back of this book. He also opened up the battle on a second front, using a good old fashioned letter, with a copy sent to the company's Managing Director. He got a full refund.

GROUP COMBAT – GANGING UP ON THE BAD GUYS

However big and powerful the organisation you're taking on, it's important to show no fear, though this could be easier said than done. They may be huge, awash with lawyers and money and with all the scruples of a fairground hustler. You, on the other hand, are just the man or woman in the street and probably a bit too fair-minded for your own good.

Nothing brings more power to our punches than knowing we are not acting in isolation and nothing scares a big bully more than seeing a group of like-minded citizens willing to fight back.

It's easier than ever to engage in group combat, thanks to the internet. Here are just some of the ways you can go about it:

USER REVIEW WEBSITES

Money Fight Club members not only go into battle for themselves, they also try to prevent others falling victim to the same scams and poor deals. User review websites are where people like you can publicise your views and complaints about a company.

Probably one of the best known is TripAdvisor (**www.tripadvisor.co.uk**) – it is used by holidaymakers to post both good and bad reviews of hotels, restaurants, resorts, etc. Another is Review Centre (**ReviewCentre.com**), which covers topics including cars, shops and insurance. To find user review groups try searching with the term: 'user reviews complaints [name of firm]'.

SOCIAL MEDIA

You may not be a regular user of Twitter and Facebook but lots of big companies use these sites to publicise their products and brands.

Businesses hate it when people post uncomplimentary reviews and remarks via these media as one person's complaint can be seen by many people. Sometimes you will get a response via Twitter far faster than if you sent an organisation an email or letter for precisely this reason. By posting your comments publicly online like this you are also helping out your fellow members of Money Fight Club by making them aware of the problems you have had with particular firms and services. Why not give it a go? Do beware the laws of defamation – your views must be reasonable and provable.

USER GROUPS AND REVIEWS OFFLINE

Check out news stories about the business or organisation you have in your sights as it could be that you are not alone. If there's been a major failure, or a large financial cock-up, there will often be articles in newspapers and features on radio and television.

Journalists will often mention consumer and action groups that are involved in a particular fight as part of their write-up of the story and you may be able to track down the group once you know its name. You can try ringing a newspaper or local radio and ask if they can put you in contact with an action group. Or start an action group of your own with a little publicity.

It's also worth talking to local offices for trading standards, money advice and consumer advice. Your local library can be a valuable source of information about consumer groups and how to contact them.

CLAIMS MANAGERS AND NO WIN-NO FEE – TREAD WARILY

There are a huge number of organisations out there that will offer to represent you in a fight for compensation for an injury, or more recently groups have been cropping up that offer to help with mis-sold payment protection insurance and other financial products. Some might be useful – a great many are not. You may face high costs if you do win and you may also have to pay the firm's expenses if you don't win.

The proliferation of no win-no fee firms has come with a hidden cost. The opportunist and spurious whiplash injury claims championed by the most dubious of these firms actually pushed car insurance premiums up. In 2013 the AA reported premiums had fallen for the first time since it had started tracking them in 1994 and this was due, at least in part, to a crackdown on rogue claims firms.

Don't pay someone to do something you're perfectly capable of doing yourself, if you have a genuine case. Some of the ads you see on TV are actually for intermediary firms that sell on your claim to a legal firm for a fee. Or they are claims managers rather than lawyers. Plus the fees they do exact on winning can be up to 50% of the compensation you're awarded.

We've already mentioned how irritating it can be to be cold-called by companies like these. You may want to take a leaf out of Richard Herman's book. Never, ever agree to let a firm act on your behalf because they called you out of the blue or you spotted some of their advertising.

MIND YOUR MANNERS

Whether you're talking to someone in person, on the phone, in a letter or email, or posting a review on a public site, mind your manners. Being polite doesn't mean appearing weak. Emotionless, controlled, good manners can be very scary.

You may be furious and badly wronged but make sure that whatever you say can be proven and is 100% accurate. Exaggerating or being personally rude can weaken your case and even leave you liable to legal action. Don't get emotional – ACT!

Accurate: For example, don't just say: "The hotel room was disgusting." Instead, you could say: "My room had not been cleaned, there were used tissues under the bed, the bedding smelt musty and the glasses were smeared and sticky to the touch." Ideally, take a picture.

Calm: Never start a conversation or send anything that you wrote when you were angry. Re-read what you wrote when you've cooled down and check it for accuracy. Count to ten before you speak. A good pause can also be intimidating.

Timely: Get cracking sooner rather than later. The longer the time that has elapsed since the event the weaker your position. Sometimes there are legal time limits. Even if there are not, people might wonder why it took you so long to complain. You may also weaken your legal case if you don't give an organisation the opportunity to put things right *at the time* – for example, if you fail to tell a resort rep how bad your holiday is while you're still there you may be in a weak position if you make a complaint later.

LIBEL AND SLANDER

If you say something derogatory about a person or organisation that isn't true (or can't be proven) it's called defamation. If you write it down and publish it, that's libel. If you say it publicly – for example, in a crowded store or office and surrounded by other people – that's slander. You could be threatened with court action and be made to pay damages if the case against you is proven. So always take care. Money Fight Club is highly disciplined. We land some heavyweight punches but we stick to the *Marquess of Queensberry Rules* and treat opponents with respect.

YOUR RIGHTS – ADDING EXTRA PUNCH

"Yo, don't I got some rights?"

ROCKY BALBOA, ROCKY 6

Knowing your rights helps you to land a tougher punch. Quoting the law, showing you know who a particular industry's regulator is, and demonstrating you can find your way around both internal and external complaints' procedures will make most companies break out in a cold sweat.

At the time of writing an overhaul of consumer law has been promised, but in the meantime there's an assortment of existing legislation on your side, as well as regulators looking out for the consumer and also the option of pursuing a small claim through the courts.

You need to take a strategic approach. There's no point in being unnecessarily aggressive without first trying a politely worded letter, which might do the trick just as well. Plus, you need to work through your options in order. For example, not giving a company the opportunity to put things right may actually weaken your case in law and most regulators won't step in until you have exhausted a firm's internal complaints procedure.

You'll find a quick guide to legislation, regulators and going to court in the Appendices at the back of this book and the very latest updates and information about new legislation on our website **www.moneyfightclub.com**.

Nearly every complaint should broadly follow a similar pattern – the combination of tactics and body blows outlined below will help you stand up to any organisation that's trying to take you for a ride:

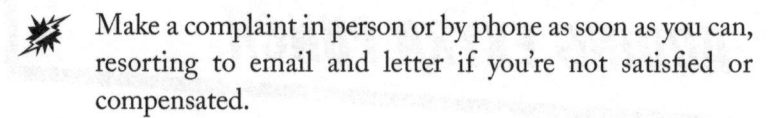

- Make a complaint in person or by phone as soon as you can, resorting to email and letter if you're not satisfied or compensated.

- If that doesn't work, or you feel you're being stalled, given the run around, or offered an inadequate resolution, formally request that the organisation move to its official complaints procedure. This should include a clear set of steps and deadlines. Make sure you understand them and keep the company to them.

- Once the internal process is exhausted and if you're still not satisfied, you can approach the organisation that regulates that particular industry or service. Again, you may threaten to move to this stage if you feel the internal process described above is being dragged out or is being approached in a half-hearted manner.

- In some cases, and depending on the amount of money involved, you may consider the courts. Keep in mind that anything above the small claims court can be very expensive to pursue and no win-no fee still comes with costs.

- Listen to your inner Money Fight Club voice. Could you take things further than you have done? Are you in danger of wimping out too soon? If you answer "yes" to either of these questions, stiffen your sinews and have another go. Start or join a campaign. Send a letter to a good consumer rights page on a national newspaper, or contact a consumer radio programme. Yo! You got rights.

WHY THE GOOD GUY (OR GIRL) WINS

It's the point in the film where the action hero (or heroine), bloodied but unbowed, eyes up the villains and their weapons and raises bruised fists one more time. The odds look stacked against the goody but a few minutes later they stand victorious. That could so easily be you.

Yes, the goodies win because they're the stars of multi-million pound movies and the outcomes are often inevitable, but they really win because failure is not an option. Go into each situation assuming you are going to be victorious and imagining a successful outcome. It will give you a head start. At the end of each Round in this book there will be a short section designed to get your head in the right space to not only fight, but win.

Trust the skills you're acquiring and use them regularly. Little skirmishes will keep your skills honed for the big fights. You can use them to get an additional discount on a high street purchase by trading retailers off against each other. You can use them to battle cowboy builders and shoddy tradesmen. Movies never dwell on this but it's obvious from the goodies' well-toned muscles and practised karate kicks that they've done the training.

If you're always on the alert where money is concerned you're less likely to find yourself in a situation where you can be taken advantage of. As the star of your

“ LITTLE SKIRMISHES WILL KEEP YOUR SKILLS HONED FOR THE BIG FIGHTS. ”

personal Money Fight Club movie you walk down the mean streets ever ready to take on the bad guys. From the opening credits we know you're going to win, albeit after some pretty awesome battles.

You just have to be prepared to come out fighting more often than you have done in the past and believe that you can win.

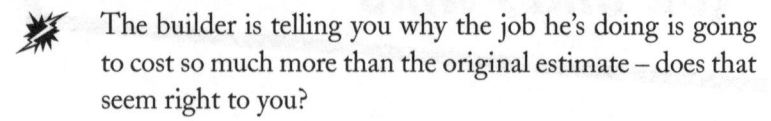

- The builder is telling you why the job he's doing is going to cost so much more than the original estimate – does that seem right to you?
- Your bank think it's your fault that the loan you took out came with insurance you could never ever claim on because you didn't qualify under its terms – are you going to accept that?
- Your car has broken down but apparently there's no way you can qualify for repairs under your extended warranty – do you just reach for your credit card?

Go with your instincts. If it feels unjust or unfair, if that's what your gut is telling you, then fight back.

- What do you feel would be the right outcome?
- Explain what you need to happen to make things right.
- Be prepared to negotiate but not to back down.

Eye up the villains and raise your financial fists. Action!

Now it's time to begin your training in earnest. All the knowledge you need is in the following pages and armed with the psychological insights you now have under your belt you can become unbeatable.

ROUND 1

FOOD WARS

CHOP!

"Happy Hunger Games! And may the odds be ever in your favour."

SUZANNE COLLINS, *THE HUNGER GAMES*

In 2012, a film based on the best-selling science fiction novel *The Hunger Games* opened and grossed $152.5m in its first weekend. The story is set in a future where the world is ruled by a rich and well-fed elite and youngsters from poor districts are chosen to fight for survival in a life and death reality TV show. A bit like the Saturday supermarket shop really.

The Hunger Games is full of unfair tricks designed to catch out the unwary, just like the neon-lit marketing nightmare that we put ourselves through to fill our cupboards and fridges.

Grandma may have headed off to the shops armed only with a wicker basket. Today you need a pocket calculator and nerves of steel. The supermarkets are out to get you. Let's see if we can stack the odds more in your favour.

At the centre of it all is how much the way we shop for food has changed. In the 1950s we shopped for food several times a week, queuing in grocers, greengrocers and butchers, buying what was seasonal and available, and often just enough for that night's meal.

Then the supermarkets arrived and while there was the benefit of choice because there was a wider variety of products on the shelves, we found ourselves buying in pre-packaged amounts that often had nothing to do with family budgets and everything to do with the economies of scale these massive food behemoths required to make their margins work.

We were tempted by out-of-season vegetables and the science of food preservation meant we could stock our cupboards and freezers with delicacies that would last months.

At the same time supermarkets began to employ increasingly sophisticated (and sometimes downright duplicitous) techniques to tempt us to part with our cash. Eye-catching end-of-aisle displays are piled high with higher-priced items (and those with the biggest profit margins). Supermarkets can also make big money from food manufacturers paying to get prime positions on the shelves for some products. They can also get a better price by threatening to de-list products.

Then, food giants were dealt a body blow by the horse meat scandal in spring 2013. A growing consumer scepticism about 'best buys' and economy lines escalated and the big brands did themselves no favours by indicating that horse meat had possibly found its way into ready meals and economy options due to consumer demand for cheap food, rather than because of any lack of concern on the part of the food industry when it came to sourcing meat.

So it's not just a question of seeking out the best deals but also making big decisions about which businesses you're willing to buy your food from and whether they deserve your trust.

PRICE HUNTING

Horse meat scandal aside, the biggest thing that drives our food shopping tactics is the need to keep within an overall budget, and the most recent UK recession has taken its toll in this respect. Figures from the Office for National Statistics (ONS) in April 2013 showed food sales down by over 4% compared with the previous month and nearly the same amount down year on year. The cold weather hit so-called summer foods but people were also pinching pennies from the table as the long winter and rising fuel prices hit their energy bills. Food prices have also been steadily increasing.

So the fighting fit food shopper goes in low. Often the best bargains are in the middle of the aisle and on the lowest shelves. If mental arithmetic isn't your strong suit take a calculator – you've probably got one on your mobile phone.

We used to be able to see the price on every can or packet, but now we have to find the price on the shelf and constantly changing offers, deals and discounts mean these may not tally with what's actually charged at the till. So keep your wits about you.

> **OFTEN THE BEST BARGAINS ARE IN THE MIDDLE OF THE AISLE AND ON THE LOWEST SHELVES.**

The game the stores play is to browbeat us into believing we're getting bargains. This includes multi-buys – such as three for the price of two, buy one get one half price, and buy this and get bonus points or vouchers. Beware! Multi-buys can work out more expensive than individual items. Big packs on special offer may still be more expensive than buying two smaller packs.

To make 'offers' appear to be better value, prices may even be higher in one branch for a few weeks so they can be 'reduced' nationwide with an advertising fanfare.

MEET A FIGHTER...

Sadly Daphne Smallman is no longer with us but it was this 78-year-old pensioner whose sharp eyes resulted in Tesco paying a £300,000 court fine for claiming that its £1.99 punnet of strawberries was 'half price'. When Daphne queried this the store remained remarkably silent on whether the fruit had ever been offered at £2.99 or £3.99 as the promotion claimed.

She got local trading standards officials involved and eventually a judge at Birmingham Crown Court imposed the fine and rebuked the supermarket chain for running "a false and misleading" promotion. Whenever we query a price, check a multi-buy or question a promotion we remember Daphne.

Supermarkets, convenience stores and other high street shops that sell food purposefully make it difficult to compare prices. Fruit, for example, may come pre-priced in a bag, priced individually and sold by weight. Sometimes products will be priced in kilos, on other occasions it will be in grams.

Often loose fruit and veg will be cheaper but you need to be sure, particularly when you may be bamboozled by multi-buy deals and less than clear shelf pricing. Sometimes the best thing to do is to locate the scales and weigh your different options, but we've heard anecdotal evidence from Money Fight Club exponents that finding the scales seems to be increasingly difficult. Can't find the scales? ASK!

Another option is to vote with your feet and use your local greengrocer or street market for fruit and vegetables. Voting with your feet in whatever situation is the Money Fight Club equivalent of kick-boxing.

Take a tip from granny, if you can, and don't buy all your shopping in one place. Supermarkets aim to profit by selling some items cheap but operating higher margins on a whole range of other shopping staples. In other words when they cut one price they increase two others. You may not be able to visit more than one supermarket every week but what about varying where you shop week by week and then buying only those items you know are genuinely cheaper in that store?

Check out bargain outlets such as Poundland and 99p Stores for staples like cleaning products. As a Money Fight Club member you keep your weekly receipts and build up a picture of what's generally cheaper where. Of course, don't believe that just because a store's name includes words like cheap, bargain, or pound that what's sold there is automatically good value.

❝WHEN THEY CUT ONE PRICE THEY INCREASE TWO OTHERS.❞

Discount stores have come under the spotlight for encouraging producers to supply them with smaller packs and jars so that products look better value than the ones elsewhere but they actually contain less. They also use big pack and poster promotions, such as "25% extra free" when the actual cost and value is no different (or maybe even worse) than that available in other retail outlets. Don't be lulled into a false sense of security.

FOOD FIGHTER TACTICS

Here are the top tactics to employ when shopping for food:

Don't be drawn in by the advertising. Be wary of the big promotions and newspaper or television advertisements designed to lure us into stores. The highly publicised and eye-catching reductions are likely to be offset by increases elsewhere.

Think about where you shop. Many supermarkets operate different prices in different stores. They may claim the costs of a smaller inner city store are higher than for a big out-of-town location, but often pricing has more to do with what the local market will tolerate (including people without cars who can't drive to out of town locations) and how much competition there is. Research published in *The Grocer* and the *Daily Mail* in May 2013 highlighted a survey from a retail consultancy that indicated convenience food shopping was generally around 10% – and could even be as much as 40% – more expensive than in a superstore.

Shop like your granny. Make a list and keep to it. Plan meals before you shop and choose recipes or mealtime favourites that enable you to use ingredients that will go off first, or while they're still fresh – such as leafy green veg. Don't change your mind.

Allow yourself time to shop, double-check prices and don't grab things from aisle ends without thinking. The stores locate their 'special offers' at aisle ends for their benefit, not yours, and as part of the complex promotional deals they strike with suppliers. If you can't see what you're looking for – ask.

As we mentioned earlier, **watch out for deceptive packaging**. Manufacturers can make their products in whatever size packs the supermarkets want. They want different sizes because they are trying to fool us into believing that we are getting good value. It means that when you visit different stores or see a 'bargain' offer in your usual store you must check exactly what you're getting for your money. The cheaper packs are likely to contain a lot less.

Manufacturers are also reducing the amount we get for our money on a regular basis to disguise their rising prices. Chocolate bars, loo rolls, cereals, cleaning products and many more are all shrinking – year on year. Packaging can cleverly disguise how little content it contains. Consider boycotting the smaller sizes or writing to the manufacturer making it clear you are not fooled. You may get some vouchers to counter the price increase.

MEET A FIGHTER...

Jo Swinson is MP for East Dunbartonshire and has spent years squaring up to Easter Egg manufacturers and their excessive use of packaging. She spotted how little room inside big, fancy Easter Egg boxes actually has Easter Egg in it.

Her annual Easter Egg report showed that, on average, Easter Eggs in 2009 took up 40% of the volume of their packaging – the best figure since the study began in 2007. But in the following three years this went down to 36% in 2010 and 38% in 2011 and 2012.

If you spot a con, make a note of it. Most of us have cameras on our mobile phones so what about photographing the offer and drawing it to the attention of the store that's trying to get you to pay more for less? One of the worst examples of this is stores where packs have "25% extra free" emblazoned on them but which are actually selling for the same price as in other stores that don't have

❝ MANUFACTURERS ARE ALSO REDUCING THE AMOUNT WE GET FOR OUR MONEY ON A REGULAR BASIS TO DISGUISE THEIR RISING PRICES. ❞

the on-pack promotion. It happens all the time. We're sick of it and you should be too. If we show stores that we're wise to their tricks maybe they'll stop.

Read all offers and promotions very carefully. A big sign may look attractive but the 'bargain' is often an addition to the range, such as a new flavour, rather than the most commonly bought version. Again, if you spot a con don't just avoid it – point it out. Let's see if we can get the big stores to play fair.

Don't automatically go for multi-buy fresh fruits and vegetables. You're unlikely to eat them all before they go off unless you have a large family or extra people staying.

If there's a good street market near you, use it. You can usually buy exactly the quantity you want and it's likely to be cheaper. Even more expensive farmers' markets can be cheaper than supermarkets for local produce in season and the food should be fresher and better quality. Get to know and build relationships with friendly stall holders selling the best quality produce and those willing to try new produce in response to customer requests. Unlike supermarkets, **loyalty counts with the local fruit and veg merchant** – it will value repeat custom and towards the end of the day will offer extra for your money.

Bigger markets also sell meat, fish and cheese. It's worth befriending the local baker, butcher and fishmonger and forming a relationship. It takes a little more time, but can save you money as well as giving you better quality food. Local shops will sell in quantities that supermarkets hate – one pork chop, a small piece of haddock and only enough cheese for tomorrow's pasta dish.

Remember **the supermarkets are not your friend** and they sell at the highest profit margin they can get away with. Their annual financial statements show that even when their sales fall their profits often rise.

When you are shopping in a supermarket, watch everything when it goes through the checkout and query anything that's more expensive than you expected it to be. Don't be embarrassed if it's marked at half-price on the shelf but then goes through the till at full price. Speak up. In fact, wherever you shop for food keep a rough tally in your head of what the total bill should be to make sure you and the shopkeeper are on the same page.

> **WATCH EVERYTHING WHEN IT GOES THROUGH THE CHECKOUT AND QUERY ANYTHING THAT'S MORE EXPENSIVE THAN YOU EXPECTED IT TO BE.**

Shop in an area where there's plenty of choice. Play the supermarket giants off against each other. An area which has a Sainsbury's, Asda, Morrisons and Tesco quite close to each other tends to offer better prices than an area where there's just one main supermarket, or a fair distance to travel between competitors. Don't be afraid to march into your local store armed with ads and promotions for other shops and point out any price differences. You may end up a winner.

VOUCHERS – DOUBLE-EDGED SWORDS

Use money-off vouchers cautiously. It's worth keeping the ones for products you use regularly in your bag, wallet or purse so they're with you when you shop. But be careful. The detergent you bought last week for £6 may be higher in price during the week when you have a voucher for £1.50 off.

Voucher websites, such as **supersavvyme.co.uk, savoo.co.uk** or **freestuff.co.uk**, can be useful and the in-house supermarket magazines also offer vouchers, but you should only use vouchers for brands you like. Some people become extreme voucher users but it's not a bargain if it sits in the cupboard unused. If you do have a lot of vouchers it's better to shop when the supermarket is likely to be less busy so that you do not end up with a queue of irritated shoppers behind you. Exchange vouchers you don't intend to use with friends – something you're not keen on may be someone else's firm favourite.

Do not be embarrassed to get your vouchers out. We find that while supermarkets may seethe at canny vouchering, the sales assistants on the tills tend to be very happy when a customer is getting a bargain. They're likely to congratulate you for being savvy.

MEET A FIGHTER...

A couple of years ago Judith Wenban from Gravesend was highlighted in the newspapers as Britain's queen of 'extreme couponing' – that's what the Americans call someone who makes the most of money-off coupons and vouchers.

She appeared on television finally paying just £5.50 for a basket of items actually totalling £65.05 and claimed her average monthly shopping bill is around £50.

Never spend more to get a bargain. Spending £60 to get 300 extra points or 5p off a litre of petrol isn't a saving if you usually only spend £45 when you shop. The supermarkets set the targets above your normal weekly spend to get you to spend more. The nearest filling station where you can get the cheap petrol may be miles away, so that any reduction is offset by the petrol used.

> **NEVER SPEND MORE TO GET A BARGAIN.**

Some supermarkets now provide little vouchers that tell us how much cheaper we could have bought our groceries elsewhere and then they sucker us into going back to them by saying they'll reduce our next shop by the amount we have overpaid. Do not go back to the store just to get the money off, but if you do go back regularly make sure you take the voucher. You might decide to go to its rival store to compare prices, though.

When you get money-off coupons at the till consider going through them there and then and handing the useless ones in at customer services on the way out. This may encourage companies to take the hint that we won't use unwanted vouchers.

CASH-BACK CARDS

Some supermarkets issue credit cards that offer either 5% cash-back or £5 when you spend a certain amount every month. These offers are often limited to the first three months and can tempt you into thinking you're saving money when you're spending more. Some bank cards offer cash-back on supermarket shopping but the amounts paid are small and should not influence what you buy. They are only good value if they don't change your shopping patterns and you don't have to pay to get the card in the first place.

NEVER TRUST A TILL

Make sure offers and multi-buys are taken off at the till. Very few supermarkets remind customers of offers at the checkout. We wonder why?

Be particularly on your guard when using self-service tills. The glitches that often arise when using self-service checkouts can cost us dear because we forget to use vouchers or don't know how to do so. Also we concentrate so hard on clearing items from the bagging area and paying, it's easy not to notice if we're charged the wrong price or don't get the multi-buy offer. Stay alert or queue for a service till.

KEEP YOUR RECEIPTS

It's surprising how often you need your receipt. You may notice something is past its use-by date after you get it home, or it looks a little dodgy, or doesn't last as long as it should. Or you realise you've bought the shower gel your teenager doesn't like. Take these things back to the in-store help desk. Fighters never use the words: "I can't be bothered." Ideally, inspect everything thoroughly before you put it in your basket and check receipts before leaving the store.

OFFERS AND UNIT PRICING

Watch out for **lack of clarity in pricing of special offers**. Legislation in the UK does not include special offers in the legal requirement to give the price per 100 grams or 100ml or per item. This can make comparison very difficult when, for example, the price is given for one can and you're buying three for the price of two. Also, smaller stores and those with a smaller range of products escape the legislation. There are moves to get the legislation changed to make comparisons easy wherever you shop, but until then you have to be careful.

It is made harder by the fact that not all shops comply with the legislation as fully as they could. If your store is confusing on unit pricing bring it to the attention of the store manager. The quicker the big stores cotton on to the fact that we're not falling for their tricks, the sooner they will have to change.

Don't be brand loyal. Try own-brand, discount and budget lines. Own-brand products are often made by the same manufacturer as the big brands and all the supermarkets now offer basic ranges but bank on enough of us still opting for the big brand. Try the basic alternative. Your family may not notice the difference but your wallet will. If the budget version doesn't do the job as well, cross it off your list forever and let the store know their budget product is no good.

Take care with 'almost out-of-date' bargains. Only buy these if they're things you like and can use immediately (or freeze) and don't be tyrannised by use-by dates. Instead, take care that fresh produce is in peak condition when you buy to extend its life in your home. The 'sniff test' is as important – don't just go by the date on the packet. Is the veg green and firm? Before use-by and sell-by dates were invented we used our noses and eyes to check out food. If you're dissatisfied, don't buy – stop an assistant and tell them the produce isn't as fresh as it should be. Also, when you get home stack your fridge and cupboards so that the oldest produce is at the front and will be used first.

Check the price per size and don't grab your preferred size without looking at others on the shelf. The bargains are often for the less popular quantities. For example, dishwasher tablets seem to come in half a dozen different pack sizes and the price per tablet can vary greatly. It may be much cheaper to buy three small boxes than one large one.

Recognise patterns. There are certain items that are regularly sold at a bargain price every few weeks. Only buy them when they are marked down – not before. Fight Club members don't pay full price on something just to see it half price next week.

Read the labels for ingredients. Check that the actual ingredients match the weasel words on the big promotional displays and posters. For example, balsamic vinegar might contain cheap colouring. Cheap wholemeal pasta may contain very little fibre compared to a better quality product. Then you might find that your supermarket is selling bottled tap water as part of its basic range (we kid you not, this actually happened):

> "Own brand bottled still water, which is on sale for 17p for two litres, is being sold alongside global mineral water brands such

as Evian and Perrier. But Tesco's Everyday Value Still Water and Asda's Smartprice Still Water are filtered water from the mains supply, the supermarkets said last night. The cost of tap water is just a third of a penny a litre, meaning the water is being sold at a massive profit."

The Telegraph, 18 August 2012

Investigate but don't automatically buy meal promotions. Supermarkets often offer meal promotions such as main courses, side dishes and pudding for two plus a bottle of wine. If you wouldn't normally have wine or a pudding, is it a bargain?

Early bargains are not the bargains they may at first appear. Christmas crackers and Easter Eggs often appear to be at a bargain prices well in advance of when they're needed. The name of this game is to get you into the store attracted by the bargains and get you buying other things as well. If you wait and compare you may get an even better deal later on. Stores also want you to mislay early purchases or use them and then have to restock.

ONLINE FOOD SHOPPING

Too many of us feel we don't have time to shop, or think we can control our spending better online. This might not be the case, so bear the following in mind:

Don't spend more than you would in a store. The supermarkets want us to shop online. They'll offer £10 or £15 off the first internet shop so long as you spend £50. That's not a saving if you would only spend £35 in store. They also have a minimum spend for free delivery. If it's £5 for a shopping basket up to £50 then that's a 10% levy.

Always **check what the delivery costs will be** for online shopping. The cost is typically £5 for an off-peak delivery under £50 but increases for evening or weekend delivery slots (or around public holidays). The supermarkets are complaining that they still cannot make enough money from online shopping and are looking at how they might make more. Their first steps are likely to be requiring a larger shop to qualify for free delivery and higher costs for convenient delivery times.

Don't miss the special offers. If you have favourite items that you return to time and again you're less likely to find bargains online. You have to look at a whole category and check all the sizes, maybe all the brands, to find some special offers. Once you've done this you may wonder how much time you're actually saving.

Avoid buying fresh food online. If you buy fresh foodstuffs you may find you've got the older stock from the front of the shelf or even a substituted item. If you've bought a particular item because it's on special offer, it's galling to find the substitute item is full price. Accept no substitutions. Buy fresh food in store if you can. Complain the moment an order arrives if the quality is poor or the sell-by date unrealistic – for example, if you have the last delivery the night before an item goes out of date.

If you add non-grocery items to your online supermarket shop be very careful! A survey by the Centre for Economics and Business Research in 2012 found that many DVDs, CDs and video games cost more than double when bought online from a supermarket compared to other retailers, and in some cases were even more expensive than in the store.

We focused on food here but **browsing for other products online can sometimes help you save money even if you don't buy online**. For example, if you want a new fridge freezer use price comparison sites – there's a list of them in the Appendix – to search for the cheapest supplier. Often the cheapest offers will be online. Print off the details and then march into a high street shop that stocks the fridge freezer you want and ask them to match the online price. What have you got to lose?

FOOD FOR THOUGHT?

Food is one of those emotive areas. Not being able to put enough food on the table for our families is possibly one of the hardest things to deal with. Being ripped off when buying food is hitting below the belt and businesses that do this deserve no quarter. How best to channel all that Money Fight Club aggression?

One way to do this is in your bargain hunting. We're often side-tracked by multi-buys and don't make any real saving.

Instead of judging your shopping success by how many bargains you picked up, instead keep a count of how many end-of-aisle cons and heavily promoted phony deals you spot (and avoid). If we don't want three-for-the-price-of-two why don't we try just buying one? Always check your bills and use the vouchers and coupons that represent a good deal for you – not just the supermarket.

Ultimately, it's about buying food, not being sold marketing. If you can get out of the supermarket without deviating from your shopping list, pat yourself on the back.

ROUND 2

HOUSEHOLD BILLS

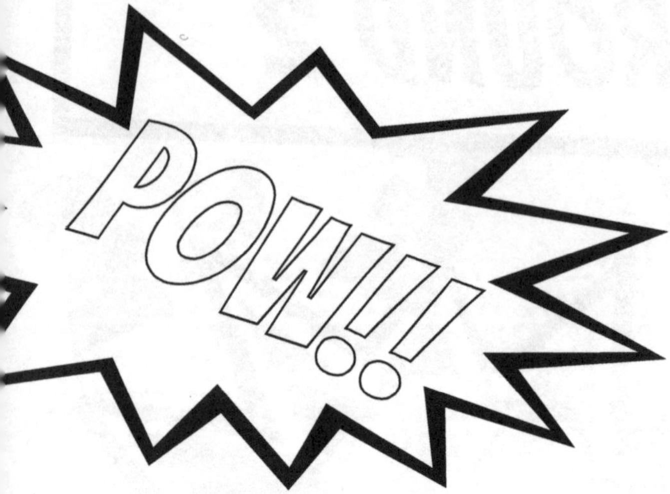
POW!!

"I go on expeditions for the same reason an estate agent sells houses – to pay the bills."

RANULPH FIENNES, ADVENTURER AND EXPLORER

Next to buying food, household bills, such as gas, electric and phone rental, are where money fighters hone their skills. These bills come thick and fast. You probably only renegotiate your mortgage every few years but you have monthly, possibly weekly, opportunities to punch above your weight around the house.

Plus this is where really big companies can get the better of us if we're not ready to fight back. They come into our home (via the letterbox) and con us – and that's plain wrong. It's even more galling because what we're dealing with here covers the real basics – such as heat and light.

Household bills have soared in recent years. According to figures released by the Bacs Family Finance Tracker at the end of 2012, we each paid out an average of £7500 in household bills in 2011. Household bills included in the figures were those where there is usually only one bill for an entire household, such as council tax, water, mortgage, TV subscription, landline phone and energy bills.

The overall total for regular bills was £11,600, including individual commitments such as mobile phone costs and things like car insurance, club memberships, life cover and personal loan repayments. For one-in-four British adults, keeping up with bill payments is the thing that concerns them most, according to Bacs.

Consumer watchdog Which? published a survey in March 2013 that found households had reduced spending by over £3000 a year, on average, since 2007 and more than 2m households had defaulted on a housing or bill payment in the preceding two months.

Staying on top of your bills is difficult and even attempts by the government to simplify things seem to make little difference. For example, towards the end of 2012 the government announced that it wanted energy companies to make changes so that they were compelled to offer customers the cheapest tariff.

Working towards this, in the spring of 2013 Ofgem, the energy regulator, came up with proposals restricting providers to offering just four tariffs each for gas and electricity. Worryingly, critics say that suppliers – and there are about 16 – could still come up with variations based on the basic four, leading to about 1000 permutations. All right, that's less than the 4000 permutations offered under the old system, but it's still a heck of a minefield for the average consumer.

There are also so many more bills to deal with these days. To our parents and grandparents, the number of things we regard as household necessities would seem extraordinary; modern life has created a whole new range of essentials. Take broadband. Most of us regard internet access of a reasonable speed as essential. At the same time, a survey published last year by thinkbroadband, an independent broadband news and information site, found that 14% of users struggled to pay for their broadband connection from household budgets.

A lot of people have their broadband bundled with other services, such as phone or TV, but this bundling then becomes one reason why people don't change providers to save money as it makes moving more complicated.

GAS AND ELECTRIC

We'll start by attacking gas and electricity companies because their bills are such a large part of our household running costs and knockout savings can be made, if you know how. These costs are on the rise again (along with energy company profits). At the same time there are changes in the pipeline which will affect how energy providers organise their tariffs, so you need to have your wits about you.

It used to be that there were regional suppliers of gas and electricity and they charged most domestic users the same amount per unit used, plus a standing charge to cover the cost of providing the service. It was easy to understand the bills.

Since the privatisation of these services in the 1980s things have changed for the worse. Competition was supposed to cut our costs but, instead, it has pushed up the profits of suppliers.

We can buy gas and electricity from any of the companies wherever we live and there are different tariffs and options. Many of the utility companies are now owned by European conglomerates and they all want us to take both services – gas and electric – from them. You should not assume that dual fuel will work out cheaper though.

You may also find your energy company promises to tell you if you would be better off with another deal or supplier – but always, always do your own research. If you discover their recommendation was wrong go back and give them a hard time – even if you spotted this before any harm was done.

There are changes promised in the Energy Bill that was working its way through parliament during 2013 but don't hold your breath. The legislative wheels grind slowly – like a punch-drunk boxer who has seen better days. In addition, the Labour Party has promised to freeze energy costs if they win the 2015 election, but this may be easier said than done. Anyway, as we mentioned earlier, the tariffs currently available leave too much room for confusion.

DO YOU KNOW WHAT YOU'RE PAYING FOR AT THE MOMENT?

The first thing you need to do is get your previous bills out and check what you've paid and how much electricity and gas was used. If you can't understand your bill ring up your supplier and get them to explain every last line of it.

A survey from uSwitch published in June 2013 showed that 70% of consumers had been overcharged on at least one household bill in the previous 12 months. The average overcharge was £196 and it was most commonly caused by charges being added when they should not have been or by the company using the wrong tariff. You must be on your guard.

Check if the bills or any documentation tells you what you should be charged per unit. Make sure you are not being charged more than this and also use the unit cost to compare with other suppliers. It's worth putting an hour or so aside to do this as the companies make it very difficult to compare charges. Again, bend your supplier's ear if you can't find what you're looking for in the paperwork.

You should also check whether the figures on your meter tally with the ones on your most recent bill. Infrequent meter readings often result in bills that are too high or, even worse, too low. If you have underpaid then at some point in the future you will have a large bill to pay to catch up with what you have used.

Get into the habit of doing a meter reading every time you get a bill, or more frequently if you are on a tight budget and cannot afford any shocks. If you know your meter reading is different to the one on your bill you should call your energy company to tell them. Some companies allow you to sign in to your account online as regularly as you wish to input your most recent meter readings. This will put you in control of the bill because you know what you're using. It will also ensure that you don't get grossly overestimated bills to leave you out of pocket, or massive underestimations followed by enormous balancing bills in the future.

It also allows you to work out what patterns increase your usage. No one is suggesting getting rid of the Christmas lights but, for example, tumble dryers typically cost upwards of 50p a load so drying outside on a fine day is very cost-effective. Consider every saving you make as getting one back on the energy companies. Our energy costs are set to keep on rising so the more energy-efficient we become the better.

If you feel in control of your usage you will feel more empowered to query energy bills with suppliers. Don't assume that just because it's their business they get it right. Remember, seven out of ten of us get an incorrect bill every year. If they've got it wrong go after them for compensation – not just your money back.

> **CONSIDER EVERY SAVING YOU MAKE AS GETTING ONE BACK ON THE ENERGY COMPANIES.**

As a rule of thumb it's cheaper to pay monthly by direct debit. Expect a discount of around 5% for paying this way. Some suppliers may also offer cash-back deals.

If you pay by direct debit it can also smooth the cost of your energy consumption across the year. In the summer your account will be in credit, proving a cushion against higher winter consumption. That said, you don't want to be too much in credit so keep an eye on your balance with the supplier to make sure it isn't building up too high. Check letters that come from your supplier as they may want to increase what they take from you and they have to tell you in advance. Often they want to take more than is entirely necessary to cover your energy usage. Don't just settle for this – negotiate.

The most expensive tariffs tend to be for those customers who have to use pre-payment meters, but it is still possible to save by switching. You may even be able to pay monthly and save more – call your supplier to ask.

HOW HUNGRY ARE YOUR APPLIANCES?

Check your appliances to see how much energy they use. Newer appliances will give the power consumption on the label in either kW or 1000 watts (so check before you buy them, particularly for appliances such as fridges which are on all the time).

If the appliance uses 1kwh it uses one unit every 60 minutes. A 100 watt light uses one unit every 10 hours whereas a one-bar electric fire uses one unit every hour it's on, and is therefore very expensive to operate. When you buy new appliances go for ones with good energy ratings.

Work out what gas and electricity you should be using each week by calculating what appliances you use and for how long, then check whether the meter agrees. Occasionally customers have faulty meters that aren't recording usage accurately. Alternatively, it may be obvious to you that an old piece of equipment is skewing the usage, in which case it could be worth buying a new appliance now for savings in the long term.

ENERGY SAVING TIPS

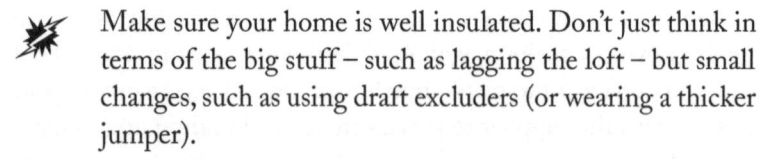

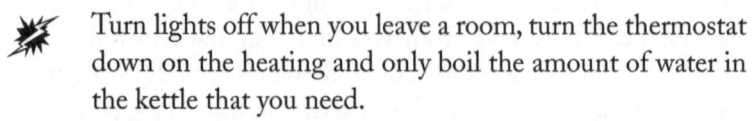

- Make sure your home is well insulated. Don't just think in terms of the big stuff – such as lagging the loft – but small changes, such as using draft excluders (or wearing a thicker jumper).

- Turn lights off when you leave a room, turn the thermostat down on the heating and only boil the amount of water in the kettle that you need.

- Waiting until your dishwasher is full or the washing machine is a full load will cut your bills, as will using the energy-efficient programmes.

- Avoid standby and pause settings. Video games played on big screens are high users of energy because the games are played for hours on end, but even worse is when the screens are paused and continue to burn energy when the games are not being played.

- Defrost your fridge and freezer regularly. If they're iced up they work less efficiently. Make sure they are on the correct setting – not on max.

TARIFFS, DEALS AND FIXES

Make sure you're paying the best tariff with the right company for your pattern of usage. You can save upwards of £300 a year by switching providers and there are often introductory and internet-only deals, or cash-back offers you can take advantage of when you move companies. Take care as the process of moving suppliers is one of those times when energy companies seem to go out of their way to mess things up. Keep an eye on things.

Most energy suppliers now offer tariffs where the energy price is fixed for a set period. These are usually more expensive than non-fixed tariffs at the outset but do afford a degree of protection against fuel price inflation. Given the way energy bills have been rising dramatically in recent years – by around 9% annually – a fixed deal may be the best deal for most, but still shop around between providers for the best one on offer.

Always take the initiative. Don't go with a deal just because it's being publicised by an energy company or features in an eye-catching advert.

USE PRICE COMPARISON WEBSITES

You should use price comparison websites to help you decide which supplier will work out best for you. You may want to try more than one site. You'll find a list in the Appendices at the back of this book but for the most up-to-date information visit our website **www.moneyfightclub.com**.

Comparison websites make money by receiving commission for new customers from the utility companies. If you go direct to a utility company rather than via one of these sites ask for cash-back. You can still use the comparison website to compare various suppliers, but once you have the information contact the supplier separately.

ENERGY FROM SUPERMARKETS AND OTHER HIGH STREET RETAILERS

If you have your energy supplied by a supermarket or high street retailer the fuel actually comes from utility companies and the retailer has just added their name to the package. The supermarket needs to make a profit from the deal as well as the actual supplier, which makes cost savings less likely in the long term – once any introductory offer has finished. Unless you have details of your exact electricity and gas usage with you when you sign up, their claims you can save hundreds of pounds a year are just guesswork.

MOVING SUPPLIER

If you owe money to your current energy company, it will usually have to be paid off before you can transfer to another supplier, but there are some exceptions. If you owe money because their readings or estimates have been wrong then you can move companies and then pay off the money.

- If you have a pre-payment meter you can transfer debts of up to £500 and then ask for a cheaper tariff when the debt is cleared.
- If your debt is less than 28 days old you should be able to move.
- If the company has just increased their prices you can have 30 days to pay off the debt and the company should not charge you the new higher tariff either.
- Most customers who try to move when in debt will find they are "debt-blocked". This is another reason to regularly check your usage and bills tally.
- If you've built up credit, this should be paid back shortly after you change company. Always keep an eye on this and check what will happen before you move.
- Keep a record of your final energy readings with your old supplier when you move. Take a photograph of the meters with a digital camera, which should also log the date and time of the photo.

INSURANCE AND WARRANTIES

Utility companies will try to sell you expensive insurance policies for your heating system and your appliances to get even more of your money. They know we all dread the boiler breaking down when it's cold outside.

Unfortunately if you lose heating and hot water on the coldest day of the year you will still wait for repairs unless you have a baby, elderly person or someone who is very ill in your household. Before you even consider paying for cover, research boiler reliability and find recommendations from other customers. Make friends with a good local plumber or heating engineer so that you know you can call on them if you have to.

COUNCIL TAX

Council tax was initially based on 1991 drive-by valuations in England and up to half a million households could be paying the wrong amount of council tax. One reason for this is that those producing the valuations often drove along roads of apparently similar properties and made visual assessments without stopping. As we all know, a group of apparently similar properties can be very different and being situated in the same road doesn't mean they are of the same value.

In addition to the initial valuation method a lot can happen in 20+ years and your secluded home may now be next to a busy road, noisy public house or abattoir, or be subject to some other property blight. In Wales the last valuation took place in 2003 so there's been less time for change.

The manner in which many properties were valued means there was plenty of scope for mistakes and if your property is the only two bedroom house in a street of bigger properties you may have been given a higher valuation than is truly merited.

The first step towards finding out is to check what band your neighbours' properties are in:

- You can check this in England and Wales by going to the website of your local listing officer at **www.voa.gov.uk**.
- In Scotland you need to check the records of the local assessor on **www.saa.gov.uk**.

Put in your postcode – you'll find which of the eight council tax bands from A to H your neighbours' homes have been put in. If they are all lower than yours – or if they are the same and you know these are more expensive houses than yours for one reason or another – then you have the beginning of a case for a reassessment. You need to review this carefully before you take action because it's possible for the council to reassess you into a higher band. The table below shows the council tax bands for the UK.

COUNCIL TAX BANDS

ENGLAND	SCOTLAND	WALES
A under £40,000	under £27,000	up to £44,000
B £40,000 to £52,000	£27,001 to £35,000	£44,000 to £65,000
C £52,001 to £68,000	£35,001 to £45,000	£65,000 to £91,000
D £68,001 to £88,000	£45,001 to £58,000	£91,000 to £123,000
E £88,001 to £120,000	£58,001 to £80,000	£123,000 to £162,000
F £120,001 to £160,000	£80,001 to £106,000	£162,000 to £223,000
G £160,001 to £320,000	£106,001 to £212,000	£223,000 to £324,000
H over £320,000	over £212,000	£324,000 to £424,000
I		over £424,000

The records will show if your neighbours have carried out improvements that are not included in the current tax band. If they've built extensions or opened up the loft space, the chances are their tax band will not have been increased, but when they come to sell the property it will be reassessed. So if their band is lower than yours but the house is larger and has a swimming pool it may not help your case as the property may be already logged to move up a band or two.

It's usually easier for owner-occupiers to challenge valuations as they are more likely to know what improvements have been made to a property since the original council tax valuation, but rental tenants can also ask for a reassessment of the band they are in. Again the first step is to check what tax bands other properties in the immediate area are in.

The best evidence you can present is the price of your home in 1991 in England and Scotland, and 2003 in Wales, and then use this to argue how your house was worth less than other houses near to it that were given the same band.

You may have the price of your property on the deeds each time it has been sold. You may be able to get a guide price for 1991 through some of the property valuation websites. Another source of information is newspaper archives that will show what prices houses in your area were being advertised for in 1991 or 2003. Real historical prices cannot be disputed.

If the council agrees that your property is in too high a band you may get a refund for as long as you have lived at the property and the future bills will be reduced as well. This can be hundreds of pounds.

A revaluation was planned by the previous Labour government to make Council tax fairer but this was abandoned by the Lib-Con coalition to save money. With so many properties today worth more than the upper limit it is likely that in the future the bands will be extended so that the multi-million pound households will pay a more proportionate level of council tax.

DISCOUNTS, REDUCTIONS AND WAIVERS

There are a number of other ways of reducing your council tax:

- Students, student nurses, certain apprentices and certain trainees do not pay council tax.
- If you live alone you're eligible for a 25% discount.
- If you live with someone other than a spouse or partner who is on a low income you should be eligible for a 25% discount. If the owner/tenant receives disability living allowance or its replacement, personal independence payments, and their resident career is not their spouse or partner then a 25% discount may apply.
- If the property has been adapted for use by a disabled person you may be able to get the council tax reduced by one band and if your property is in band A you will get a reduction of one-sixth of the tax.
- If you live in a property in which the landlord is resident then the landlord is liable for the council tax.
- If you're a tenant in a property in multiple-occupation with shared rooms then the landlord pays the council tax even if they're not resident at the property.
- If a property is unoccupied and unfurnished then no council tax is paid for six months. This exemption can be extended to 12 months if significant repairs are being undertaken.
- If a property is empty because the owner/tenant is in prison/hospital or a care home then no council tax is due.
- Owners or renters of second homes in England can get a discount of up to 50% on this second property, but most councils only give a council tax discount of 10% and even these discounts are being withdrawn. In Wales the discounts can be 50%, 25% or nothing at all. In Scotland holiday homes attract council tax of 90% of the valuation.

- Local authorities can also reduce council tax to nil in cases of hardship or when a property is affected by an event such as flooding. Applications should be sent to the chief executive of the council. It is worth asking, but these concessions are also being withdrawn.

- Council tax support can be applied for through the housing department of a council by those on low incomes if they have less than £16,000 in savings. Those who get the pension credit guarantee can get council tax support unless they live with other adults. Those who are working can get help with their council tax if their housing costs and outgoings are high compared to their income. Once again, councils are cutting back on this help, but it is worth investigating.

WATER

Water costs used to be small before the privatisation of the supply industry in 1990. The average annual cost of water has increased by about 50% since privatisation, to £356 per year by 2010/11. Now water can be a major outlay, with people living in some parts of the country paying substantially more for the same consumption than in other areas. You can't change supplier, but you can still square up to them and find ways to reduce what you're paying.

You also have a pretty powerful ally in your corner – the Consumer Council for Water (CCWater). Since being set up in 2005, CCWater has won over £14.3m in compensation for water customers, with £2.3m in compensation in 2011/12 alone.

It's also possible to save hundreds of pounds a year if you keep an eye on your water consumption, look at how you personally use water and investigate the pros and cons of having a meter.

Water companies are increasingly rolling out water meters to all households but irrespective of what your own water company is doing, it may make sense to switch to a meter sooner rather than later. It's possible to substantially reduce your consumption with a few tips and tricks, and this will then be reflected in lower meter readings. Here are some of our tried and true favourites:

- Use economy cycles on washers and dishwashers, and only wash full loads.
- Keep showers to five minutes (an egg timer in the bathroom can be helpful with teenagers).
- Make sure the shower head is efficient – you can get special eco shower heads that use less water but still give you a powerful shower.
- Do not wallow in deep baths unless something (or someone) else is going to use the water afterwards – for example, use the water to wash the car.
- Do not leave taps running to clean teeth or wash hands. Keep a jug of water in the fridge so you do not have to run the cold tap for ages to get water cold enough to drink.
- Reduce the amount of water each time you flush the loo – in the old days you used to a put a brick in the cistern but these days you can get special bags (often free from your water company).
- Keep a water butt in the garden to collect rain water for plants.

SHOULD YOU SWITCH TO A METER?

When weighing up whether to make the move to a meter, a good starting point is CCWater's online calculator (see **www.ccwater.org.uk**). Individual water companies also have their own calculators so CCWater says you should double check using the calculator provided by your supplier before moving. About 40% of families in the UK have meters but this is set to rise to 50% by 2015 and the government wants every household to be on a meter by 2020.

Ofwat, the water regulator, estimates metering can reduce household water bills by 9% to 21%, but the potential savings are greater for individuals and small families who live in large houses and don't waste any water. Large families are less likely to benefit. Check with neighbours who have meters about their usage and charges. Those who live alone or are out of the house all day should save most. Having a meter also gives you a much clearer understanding of how much water you use and encourages you to explore more ways of saving it.

If you decide against a meter but know your water company is going to make them compulsory it's worth starting to plan how you'll minimise the pain. For example, if you're buying a new washing machine or thinking of fitting a new shower, compare the water consumption of different ones – as well as energy use – before buying.

At the time of writing, if you switch to a meter and your bills turn out to be higher than your current charges you may be able to ask your water company to go back to your old way of paying, so long as you do this within a year of installation. This isn't the case with all companies, so check first. If you move to a property that already has a water meter, you can't switch to unmetered bills.

Meters in England and Wales are usually fitted for free. In Scotland the meter is provided free but the cost of creating the space for it is met by the property owner. Check for any charges before you go ahead. In England and Wales you may be charged if you want the meter located somewhere other than where the water company wants to put it.

Always check your meter regularly. When no appliances that use water are running, and all taps, etc., are off, go outside and check the dial – it should not be moving.

When a property has no water meter, water and sewerage costs are based on the rental valuations for houses in England and Wales that were used to assess rateable values up until 1990. The last full valuation was in the 1970s so many of these are out of date.

PHONES

LANDLINES

It used to be so simple. There was British Telecom and one phone plugged into a socket in the hall – that was it. Now we have phone lines and broadband, line rental and handsets. Plus many of us use alternatives such as Skype.

Yet many households still use BT as their landline provider because they haven't thought about changing or looked too closely at exactly what they're getting for their money. When Which? surveyed its members it found that nearly two-thirds felt that they ended up paying less on calls and line rental after switching providers.

It's possible to save hundreds of pounds a year on telephone calls from landlines (and mobiles), although it takes a bit of effort to make sure you're with the best company and on the right tariff. You may be better off paying one company for the phone line, another for your main calls and a third for international calls. That may sound complicated but if you're a big phone user the savings could be substantial. Even if you find the right tariff the price can change, so you need to keep your wits about you.

Skype's a very cheap way of keeping in contact with friends and family around the world. If you and the person you are calling both have Skype accounts you can call each other for free over your internet connection. You can also use Skype to call landlines and mobiles over the internet, for which you pay a charge.

There's one quick win for BT customers. With Line Rental Saver you pay for your home telephone line rental for the whole year in one payment of £141. That works out at £11.75 a month, whereas if you pay your line rental in your bill each month it works out at £15.45 per month. Paper-free billing and paying by direct debit are also ways to cut costs.

HOW TO MAKE SAVINGS

As with other major bills, a good starting point is using a price comparison site, such as **www.uswitch.com**. There is a list of comparison sites in the Appendix and check out our website for the latest information (**www.moneyfightclub.com**).

If all this sounds like hard work at least do one thing – ring up your current provider and say you're unhappy with how much things are costing and you're thinking of moving to another provider. That may be enough to get you moved on to a better price plan.

Whether you're moving to another provider or renegotiating with your existing one, always, always check what the conditions are if you decide to cancel a phone contract, or phone and broadband bundle, early. Watch out for renewable contracts that automatically sign you up for a further period without you having to do anything.

Before you can make any other savings you need to know what your call patterns are and what you get for your money on your current contracts for landline and mobile. You have to make sure you use the landline when it's cheaper to do so and make calls using your mobile when it's cheaper to use that. If you don't know this already, check.

For example, you may be penalised if you make calls that last more than 60 minutes – many 'unlimited' inclusive deals limit the length of free calls to an hour. If you exceed the limit on a call then you pay, but if you put the phone down before the hour is up and call the same number again you don't pay. This is particularly worthwhile for those customers who get 'unlimited' international calls for paying a modest monthly fee.

Learn when 'evenings' start and finish for your home phone company. You might assume it is 6pm but it could be 6.30pm or even 7pm. Weekend rates may start at midnight on Friday and finish at midnight on Sunday but don't assume that's the case – check.

PREMIUM RATE NUMBERS

Watch out for the premium price phone numbers used by utility and other companies. These tend not to be included in inclusive packages and if they are there will be a limit to the number of calls that can be made for free. There are companies out there that auto dial your number and then hang up after one ring – prompting you to ring them back. The return calls could cost you 50p a minute from a BT landline. 070 numbers are a case in point.

While less scrupulous companies use the very expensive premium numbers to make money, good old banks and building societies are not totally free of shame. When NatWest's online banking was hit by a major IT failure in the summer of 2012, customers were urged to call an 0845 number – where you could easily run up a tenner on your mobile phone bill.

If you don't recognise a code check the small print on the website of the company you're calling. Call costs should also be on bills and other paperwork for the company you plan to call.

Look for allies in the phone battle. For example, **SayNoTo0870.com** will provide alternative numbers for you to call. It's also worth remembering that if the company/organisation provides a number for people to ring from outside the UK – a +44 number – this will usually be an ordinary UK number that isn't premium-rated. To use the number from within the UK all you need to do is replace the +44 with 0.

MOBILES

If landlines are complicated that's nothing compared to the mobile market. There it's not just a question of tariffs but the array of handsets on offer. While nobody will cast admiring glances at the landline handsets you have in your home (well, it's unlikely), people can get very excited about their choice of mobile. This complexity means that this is the ideal place to practice your negotiating techniques; nothing should be taken at face value. Tariffs, add-ons and phones are all open to negotiation and hard bargaining.

Let's start with the concept of a 'free' phone. It isn't. Phones are dangled like carrots, particularly when you switch providers. So before switching, or getting a new mobile phone, check out what your preferred handset costs to buy upfront in different stores and from different providers.

Find out if buying your own phone and getting a Sim-only deal will work out cheaper over 12 or 24 months. With a Sim-only deal, you want one with no tie-in, which you can just cancel at the end of any month. Some will tie you into 12-month – or longer – contracts if you don't take care.

Keep an eye on why, how often and when you use your mobile, so you don't get caught out with mobile contracts by exceeding your free or cheap contracted calls by a small margin. For example, you may get a new phone with a great little camera on it and you're suddenly using your mobile to send shots to friends and relatives. Assume that anything that's not stipulated within your contract – for example, picture messages – is going to cost you a premium. You also need to check which networks you can call as part of your 'free' minutes per month.

Changing jobs, providing children with their first mobile phone, house hunting… these are just some of the life events that can send your mobile minutes skyrocketing. You may also find your circumstances have changed and you're using less mobile minutes or texts than you used to. Don't be afraid to contact the mobile provider to renegotiate, no matter what your contract may say.

If you're getting towards the end of your contract and your usage has changed, it may make sense to buy yourself out of it rather than pay a premium price for additional usage. If your mobile operator is less than accommodating you can threaten to walk to a new one when your contract does expire.

While you may feel a fixed price is a fixed price, your mobile provider may take a distinctly different view when they're the ones trying to change things. Millions of mobile phone users are finding that their contracts to pay a 'fixed' amount every month or for fixed periods are not fixed at all, and are being increased to take account of inflation. Which? has a 'fixed means fixed' campaign and wants Ofcom to take action against the mobile giants who are increasing their prices in this way. The regulator has also ordered mobile companies to stop charging customers up to 40p a minute for dialling 0800 numbers.

If you're finding that you can't afford your package it's worth asking if you can move to a cheaper one. The companies *can* force you to stick to the small print of your contract, but they may prefer to get a smaller monthly amount from you every month rather than risk you not being able to pay your current, higher bills.

INSURANCE

Don't buy separate insurance for your mobile. When you get a new one the store will try to sell you expensive cover as this is how staff make their commission and they may have targets to sell a certain number of insurance policies every week.

A report from the Financial Conduct Authority in June 2013 found that making a successful insurance claim for a lost mobile phone could be practically impossible. It said that some policies were not designed to meet customers' needs. The insurance companies have promised to improve, but we are not holding our breath.

You should:

- Check whether your mobile is covered for theft or accidental damage on your household insurance policy.
- Find out if your bank account already offers this cover. Holiday insurance may also cover a lost or stolen phone, but not the cost of any calls made on the phone by the thief.
- Check what the excess is on the insurance policy. It may be more than the cost of a new mobile.

Report it immediately if you lose your telephone. You will be responsible for any calls made on the lost phone, so you need to put a stop to this straightaway, and the longer the time between the loss and you reporting it the more likely it is the company will think you're complicit. Always tell the police and get a crime number.

INTERNATIONAL CALLS

Take particular care when using your mobile phone abroad. You may find you can pay an additional tariff to keep holiday call costs down but make sure you know what you will be charged for. Before you go on holiday call your mobile company and find out exactly what the charges are and how to avoid them. Turn off the data roaming facility. Usually receiving texts is free and replying is relatively cheap but phone calls are expensive to receive and make, and accessing voicemail and the internet can rack costs up.

You may also want to consider buying a much cheaper second phone with less functionality – but a longer battery life – to avoid the risk of your top-of-the-range smartphone being pinched from your beach bag.

In the EU there are now fixed costs with all companies charging around 24p a minute for making calls and 7p a minute for receiving them (check with your provider), but these can still add up quickly. Further afield you can tot up hundreds of pounds in bills. Check before you travel. Mobile companies tend to be totally unsympathetic when holidaymakers are charged thousands of pounds for data use when they usually only pay, say, £20 a month at home. These cautions also hold true when using a laptop Wi-Fi dongle abroad.

There are ways of saving money on both mobile and landline international calls.

Even when you're not on holiday, making international calls from your mobile can be extremely expensive. One option is to use Rebtel (www.rebtel.com). The service routes your calls via the internet, dramatically cutting costs, particularly if both people on the call are Rebtel members. You can also use Rebtel on your landline.

Another option is **18185.co.uk**. A service such as this overrides your supplier's call charges, allowing you to make calls anywhere in the world for a fraction of the cost of the big phone companies.

In Which? surveys **18185.co.uk** scores highly for value and customer service, which is better than the main companies. You set up the account with them, make your calls using the prefix number and get a separate bill. Not all major companies allow you to use the service, but currently BT and the Post Office do. You can even get cheaper rates on 087 numbers and mobile calls using an override provider. You pay the override service for, say, international calls or calls to mobiles, and pay your main phone line provider for other calls.

08** NUMBERS

Don't call 084, 087 or 09 numbers with a mobile. These can cost you 25p a minute or more, which is a lot to spend just to listen to music as your utility company offers you different options on its automated answering system and holds you in a queue.

Beware of any small print that says how much a call will cost per minute from a BT landline but casually adds that from other networks and mobiles the call could cost "significantly more." Find out how much more before you dial that number!

VOICE OVER INTERNET

Voice over internet services, such as Skype, are a wonderful alternative to landlines and mobiles as you can also use webcams to have a video conversation and it is free if both of you are on a computer. For calls from a computer to a mobile or landline you pay as you go. A credit of £10 is likely to last you a year, even with lots of international calls.

KNOW YOUR USAGE

Here are some top tips to save you money on phones:

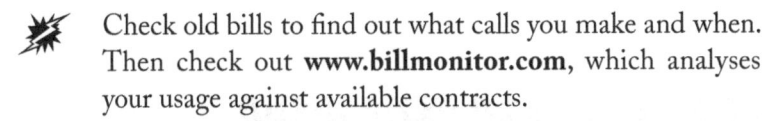

- Check old bills to find out what calls you make and when. Then check out **www.billmonitor.com**, which analyses your usage against available contracts.

- If you make very few calls on your landline then you should get a basic line rental package. You can find the current rates on price comparison sites such as **MoneySupermarket.com**. There's more about comparison sites in the Appendix.

- Check what the basic packages cover. It may be just the line, the line and weekend calls, or for a little more it may include weekend, evening calls and calls to some international destinations.

- Watch for hidden clauses. Some mobile companies sign customers up for a fixed price per month over 12, 18 or 24 months and then hide in the small print the fact that they can increase that price at will.

- Is there an additional connection fee?

- Make use of your landline at weekends when calls are generally cheaper (but check your contract).

- Watch the clock when you're chatting. Calls over 60 minutes may be excluded from inclusive deals.

- If most of your calls are to one number check if you can get free calls by signing up with the same phone company as your phone buddy.

- Check what the charges are to mobiles. If your landline is expensive or you need to call at peak times it may be that you could call and ask the person at the other end to call you back if they have plenty of unused 'free' minutes.

- Check the costs of extra services provided by phone companies as sometimes these can be positively extortionate. For example, call waiting can cost £3.30 a month from BT. That's a lot to pay for some beeps when you're already busy on the phone. An operator alarm call from a BT landline costs more than a pint down the local.

TELEVISION AND BROADBAND

The division between your computer and your TV is blurring. As well as TV packages that come via satellite you may also be looking at internet-enabled TVs that will allow you to access on-demand services such as iPlayer and paid-for options like Netflix. At the time of writing BT were sweetening their broadband deal with a free sports channel.

As a rule of thumb television contracts are always more expensive than the full-page advertisements in newspapers and flyers that come through the letterbox would lead you to expect. They always appear to be much cheaper than your current provider but somehow, during the signing up process, the contract costs grow.

Some of the price inflation is down to the extra services you may be tempted to take on, such as premium films or special sports. The chances are the package will also include broadband and a charge for line rental, which you have to pay for.

An essential skill for TV money fighting is: don't get talked into extras!

Check how many paid-for programmes, films and sporting events you actually watch. Calculate whether they are worth the monthly fee you're paying or are proposing to pay. It used to be that people compared the costs of the satellite contract with cinema attendance. Now there are plenty of other alternatives that can keep you entertained in your own home, including on-demand options from the major TV companies.

Work out for yourself if the satellite contract is good value based on what you want to watch – not just what you could watch if you had the package. It could cost as much as your monthly heating and lighting bill. Compare the value to the household.

You can save a great deal of money by opting for HD Freeview if you personally feel you have enough television options with terrestrial stations. You have to pay for a set-top box – prices start at around £140 – but that's less than three months of a typical satellite contract and will still allow you to record programmes to watch later.

Things are changing all the time. For example, YouView was launched in 2012 and had been installed in almost half a million homes by spring 2013. With YouView you can access on-demand programmes via the BBC iPlayer, ITV Player or Channel 4's 4OD. The service is available in broadband bundles with BT and TalkTalk, or set-top boxes can be purchased for around £300.

Autumn 2013 saw the launch of the Now TV box that will apparently allow non-smart TVs to access programmes over the internet. The box costs just £9.99.

If you are a football fan, check how many matches are broadcast that you will want to watch. Many football fans buy a satellite package because they want to watch their team live, but unfortunately many of the key premiership matches are not broadcast and they end up watching *Match of the Day* for edited highlights anyway. Many Champions League matches are broadcast free and live on terrestrial channels as well.

Don't be fooled by the advertisements; you may still miss the goals even if you pay a lot every month. Also watch out for satellite companies that switch sports between channels so you constantly need to change or extend your package.

CANCELLATION CHARGES

As with phones, be on your guard against cancellation charges hitting you hard if you want to get out of a contract early. Find out what it will cost to cancel your package – which could easily happen if you move house and don't need the service any more, or if your circumstances change and you cannot afford to keep it all going. Think about this before you subscribe.

TV and broadband packages are one of the areas where contracts may be automatically renewed. Phone regulator Ofcom says that providers offering renewable contracts must make the terms of the contract clear before a customer signs up. Customers must also be reminded when they're coming to the end of their contract.

HOUSEHOLD INSURANCE

Whether you own or rent you'll need to insure your home contents. Renters will usually find the building's insurance is handled by their landlord. Use price comparison websites to find the best deals – we have a list of them in the Appendix – but remember some insurers don't offer their products through such sites.

Never have your contents insurance on automatic renewal from a credit card or bank account. This leaves you open to being overcharged, as what companies charge is liable to increase and you need to keep an eye on this. Last year's competitive quote can become this year's extortionate one and it's the nature of large businesses to treat existing customers with borderline contempt while creating tempting offers to entice new customers in.

Even more dangerous is the fact that many of us change credit cards or bank accounts during the course of a year and we may forget about the insurance policy. If the payment isn't made you're then left without insurance. Less dramatic is that there may be a change in your circumstances such as buying a new piece of furniture or taking in a lodger that the insurance company will want to know about. In the case of the latter if you have a non-family member renting a room from you this could invalidate your insurance for most claims.

Even if your renewal quote looks good, check to see if your insurer is offering an even better deal for new customers. If they are, be prepared to ring them up and argue the toss. After all, you have the option of going elsewhere. It's amazing how many offers that are 'only for new customers' can actually be accessed by existing customers if they stand their ground.

While keeping premiums down is important, you also need to think about the claims service, in case you need to make use of this later. Some companies can seem incredibly cheap but when you make a claim it's like extracting teeth. Check for feedback from other people using online consumer forums and surveys from independent consumer champions such as Which?.

When you make a claim you will usually find next year's premium increases. Most policies come with an excess, the amount of any claim you pay yourself – say, the first £50. So making a small claim can work out expensive, as you only get a proportion of the claim paid out by the insurer, after the excess is taken into account.

Alternatively, going for a higher excess is one way of keeping premiums down on a range of insurances. For example, you may feel you have enough income to cover loss or damage to your home up to, say, £250, so could set your excess at that level.

FLOOD RISK

Some 5.5m homes in England and Wales are at risk of flooding. The government has set up a fund with insurers to start operating in 2015. This fund will ensure that the price of flood insurance is not excessive. It is based on council tax bands and it should mean that people at risk of flooding can get cover, although it will exclude the most expensive properties. This is another reason for checking your council tax band is not too high.

Find out whether your home is at risk by checking **www.environment-agency.gov.uk**. If your property has never been flooded and your insurer wants to increase your premiums to take account of the risk that it might, be provide all the relevant information. The insurer will usually work on postcodes and will not know your specific details.

CAN YOU HANDLE BILLS LIKE A GAZILLIONAIRE?

Okay, you wanted that shiny new mobile and now seem to be lumbered with a rubbish phone contract that seems way too high, or you want to go about changing your electricity supplier but keep getting the run around about what you owe. That boiler cover you pay for each month may prove to be as much protection as a chocolate fireguard and you should really ask for your premiums back, but, oh, it's all so tricky and just thinking about it make you go all squirmy and unsure of yourself.

There's one thing you can be sure of: You pay.

You pay the piper, the mobile company, gas provider, the water utility, the financial services provider, the supermarket… so you should get to call the tune. Companies should dance to your melody. But they don't – do they?

The fact is that all the above are bills and bills mean we 'owe' someone, so this tends to put us on the back foot. Paying what we owe is one of the ways we affirm our status. Not being able to make ends meet undermines that status. So we just keep up-to-date with the bills and struggle with the charges we don't quite understand or don't think we should be facing.

Now let's look at this situation a little differently.

Imagine you were incredibly wealthy with more money than you could spend in a thousand lifetimes. You could afford anything your little heart desired. It so happens that you owe £150 on a gas bill. How would that make you feel? Chances are you wouldn't feel very much at all; it's a small bill. You wouldn't worry because you would feel supremely confident about your ability to pay. You wouldn't be on the back foot.

Now let's imagine a slightly bigger bill for our imaginary gazillionaire. A new yacht for example, with gold taps in all four en suite bathrooms. That'll be £3.2m, thank you very much. They're still not on the back foot though. Actually, it's quite the reverse. Instead they're inspecting the yacht and making last-minute changes. Rather than gold taps they want platinum, and the master bedroom isn't big enough. Our gazillionaire knows that they've got the upper hand in the transaction. They don't need to pay the bill fast to feel good. So the question is – why can't we all handle bills like a gazillionaire?

The fact is companies that provide our household services need us. Thanks to competition we do have choices. Oh yes, these big businesses go out of their way to make deciding as hard as possible, but what does that say about them? The fact is they're scared that if it was very simple to see what we were getting for our money, some of them would go out of business overnight.

If we all vote with our feet, cut up rough on the phone, refuse to back down and wear sales people into the ground with our knowledge and incisive questioning, not only will we save money and prevent ourselves being ripped off but we'll force big businesses to change. Slowly but surely. They get away with what they do because we let them.

Bills aren't debts, they're weapons. Stay on top of them and then use them to get exactly what you want.

ROUND 3

BANKS AND FINANCE

CRACK!

"When humans go into or on to the sea, they enter the domain of the shark and do so at their own risk."

ALEX MACCORMICK, SHARK ATTACKS: TERRIFYING TRUE ACCOUNTS OF SHARK ATTACKS WORLDWIDE

The world we move in is made up of traditional sharks and cowboys who you might already be on your guard against, such as bogus builders and tradespeople, plus there is a whole new range of suited and booted financial professionals working for banks, building societies and other institutions who we think we can trust. There's blood in the water and most of it is ours.

Figures for the year to April 2013 released by the Financial Ombudsman Service revealed that 76% of the complaints the service received were about banks, up from 65.5% in the previous year. The number of people complaining to the ombudsman has been steadily rising over the years.

Complaints from other sectors, such as insurers and financial advisors, fell, with the exception of building societies who saw complaints rise to 4.5% of the total complaints received by the Ombudsman (a drop in the ocean compared to banks). Bank and building society complaints have been fuelled by the mis-selling scandal surrounding payment protection insurance (PPI).

Payment protection insurance was foisted on millions – often as a condition of taking out a loan – and it was sold to people who were unable to claim because they were self-employed, had a pre-existing medical condition, or even some who were retired.

Not only do banks treat us badly and sell us products we don't need or can't use, they also accuse us of being criminals when we are actually the victims of their faulty systems, or of fraudsters.

Customers often find they have to prove they did not withdraw money using their debit cards or did not buy items using their cards when they query rogue payments. The typical response from the financial institution concerned is that their systems are secure so therefore the customer must have been negligent, or even that they or a member of their family used the cash machine and forgot.

Bank rules demand that they give back a customer's money – unless they can prove the customer was at fault. That's why they're so keen to rattle our cage and see if they can spook us into backing down. Stand your ground. Don't be browbeaten into thinking you may be at fault or that a member of your family has stolen your money. If you know that you did not write down your PIN, fight to the end.

Fraudsters have an ever-evolving array of sophisticated techniques designed to obtain our financial details. You only have to look at how often banks have been shown up as having failing systems to know they can – and do – make mistakes with your cash.

Banks are investing in more and more virtual payment systems that are a gift to fraudsters, so it is quite often they who are at fault, not us, their customers. Contactless cards can apparently be cloned from inside a wallet and the emergency cash system operated by one bank had to be stopped after one customer, who had not applied for emergency cash, found £950 had disappeared from his account in just a couple of days.

So it's no time to pull your punches with the banks. As you fight to get even remember the way we were all ripped off over and over again:

- Excessive overdraft charges have long been in the ring with us, with the least well-off often paying most.
- The Financial Conduct Authority reported in the summer of 2013 that some 30,000 bank customers were due compensation because banks had failed to cancel regular payments to third parties when the customers asked them to.

- Rigged Libor rates were the result of UK banks providing false figures. This is likely to have increased the cost of mortgages and other loans.
- Banks tried to get rid of cheques even though millions of customers and businesses still rely on this method of payment.
- Packaged current accounts that charge you over the odds for insurance and other services you don't need are being heavily promoted by bank staff. Check what it will cost and whether you already have cheaper insurance from elsewhere.
- When they make mistakes banks refuse to admit it. Too often customers who are charged too much, sold the wrong product, have their accounts mismanaged or cheques lost cannot get compensation without a long fight.

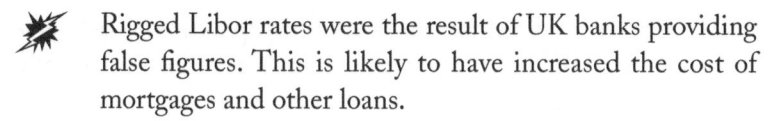

CURRENT ACCOUNTS

It's far easier to move bank accounts than it used to be. Since September 2013 we have been able to move to a new current account in seven working days. The banks must meet this schedule.

Banks aren't exactly pleased about this – they prefer us to change our bank accounts less often than our life partners. But while you may find your one true love, your relationship with your bank is no love affair and you should be willing to break up with your current choice as soon as they displease you.

> **AS YOU FIGHT TO GET EVEN REMEMBER THE WAY WE WERE ALL RIPPED OFF OVER AND OVER AGAIN.**

So many of us settle into relationships of quiet complacency with our banks; only 3% of people change bank accounts each year. The fact is it doesn't matter if they haven't gone out of their way to displease you by messing up payments or losing deposits – you should always be looking for a more financially attractive option. Consider a bit of free love. There's no reason why you can't have more than one cheque account at different banks. This is probably a sensible course after a series of computer breakdowns on the part of the major banks has left customers unable to get cash out of ATMs or use their cards.

You need to do a bit of personal research before you can compare your bank account with other bank accounts. Do you know the terms and conditions of your current account? To stand a chance of fighting back and getting the best deal you need to find these out.

The good news is that the European Commission has made it easier for us to switch accounts and compare fees. The bad news is that banks won't be able to hide costs away so easily and will probably take so-called free banking off the table.

FLOOR YOUR BANK IN 12 MOVES OR LESS

1. Do you have an authorised overdraft, know how much it is and what you're charged if you use it?

It works out expensive if you're overdrawn most days of the month, but if you don't have an overdraft limit or if you exceed the one you do have then the costs are likely to double.

2. Is your free banking really free?

We could be paying from £120 to £900 a year for our so-called free current accounts (Which? 2012). This is made up of charges and interest and then there's the matter of the banks having use of our money and often paying little or nothing on a current account in interest. So there's much to be gained by moving if you can get a better interest rate or lower charges.

3. How much are you charged to use your debit card abroad?

Most banks charge a lot for the convenience of using cash machines abroad. There's usually a fee for the transaction and the exchange rate is rubbish into the bargain. If you travel a lot it's worth choosing a bank or building society that does not charge for using cash machines abroad.

4. What rate of interest are you getting on your current account?

Some current accounts still offer interest on balances, but often this is an introductory offer, so if you moved for 5% on your current account some time ago the chances are the offer has expired and you're getting something nearer to 0.1% now.

5. How long have you had your current account?

If the answer is more than two years the chances are the bank you're with will have a better deal if you ask to switch to their latest current account designed to attract new customers. It should take only seconds to move your money over and you will retain your cash card and PIN number for the new account.

You're likely to do even better by moving to another bank. Check out financial comparison sites such as **moneyfacts.co.uk** or **moneysupermarket.com**. Many banks want your custom when they don't have it and offer £100 switching fee and interest on the current account for 12 months. There are also cash-back offers when you spend on a new account. If the cash-back is on essentials such as household bills then it's a pure gain, but if you're encouraged to buy things you wouldn't normally buy to get the cash-back then this isn't a benefit at all.

6. Do you have a packaged account that has a monthly fee?

No one chooses accounts with monthly fees; they are sold them by a counter clerk who will earn points and keep their job if they sell lots. They can cost up to £25 a month, but more generally are £10 to £15. That's £120 to £300 a year. If you're paying for such a package check what you get for it. Often it's unlimited travel insurance, legal expenses cover, mobile phone cover, or all three together.

If you're paying for these you need to make sure they are good value. Too often the travel insurance excludes the over 64s and if you only go on one holiday to Europe each year you can buy it far cheaper when you actually travel. You may even have travel insurance as part of your household insurance already, so you could be paying twice for it. Mobile phones may also be covered by your household insurance or the cover may be cheaper elsewhere.

That said, some packaged accounts offer value at the outset with an attractive rate of interest and cash-back on your regular debits, but you need to monitor over time as the terms will change and could leave you paying over the odds.

7. Have you stuck with the same bank because you cannot face changing to another and having all your direct debits and standing orders messed up?

Banks are now obliged to help you transfer your current account and all its regular payments to another bank in seven days. To be on the safe side, because competence isn't their strong suit, it's best to draw up a list of all your regular payments and check them off as they are transferred. If the transfer is done online, check the list of direct debits or regular payments in your account to make sure that everything that should be showing is listed. It's probably worth having a little cash to hand during the transfer process so that you can pay everyday items with cash – in case there is any glitch accessing your new account from ATMs, etc.

8. Do you know how much you're paying your bank for nothing?

You can pay hundreds of pounds a year even if you don't go overdrawn or have a monthly or annual fee. For example, costly levies on using a debit card overseas and calls to premium-rate telephone numbers add up quickly. What is your bank charging you? Find out, complain and threaten to move.

Many of us keep too much money in current accounts, especially when virtually no interest is paid. The fear of overdrawing and incurring hefty charges encourages customers to play safe. We need to check our accounts daily online or arrange to receive text updates of balances each morning. Then we can keep less in the account and earn more interest in a savings account until the money is actually needed.

9. Control your money, don't let it control you

You can move your monthly direct debits to be paid out after your wages have been paid in. This move costs nothing and generally can be done once. If you are often overdrawn in the days running up to your pay going into your account, it should save you money every month.

10. Be on your guard in bank branches

You're at your most vulnerable in bank branch waters. Bank staff are given targets to sell investment products and insurance and these are more likely to be linked to their pay and bonuses rather than your needs. There are moves to clamp down on this in the wake of major mis-selling, but in the meantime be on your guard.

11. Can you always use your own money when you need to?

Believe it or not if you have a substantial amount of money in your internet bank account that you need to transfer to a third party such as a solicitor for a house purchase, or a garage to pay for a car, you may find the bank will have limits that prevent you from doing this. You may not be told of these until you need to make the transfer.

To start with there's likely to be a limit on how much you can move in one transfer from your e-savings account to your cheque account. Then there are limits on transfers from your current account to a third party. Of course, when you go into the bank to arrange such a payment there may be a fee to pay if you want to do it quickly.

12. Finally, only use cash machines that are free

There are agreements between the main banks to provide free cash machines and supermarkets often offer a machine that's free to use. Elsewhere cash machines can come with hefty charges, particularly if you only want to withdraw small amounts. Small corner shops often have expensive cash machines.

SAVINGS ACCOUNTS

Savings rates in recent years have been rubbish and banks have never been more duplicitous in the way they set up savings accounts. No one can put money in a savings account and expect to get a fair deal or to be told when the rate of interest is cut.

Among the worst accounts are cash ISAs. These tax-free Individual Savings Accounts limit how much you can put in each year and while at the start of every tax year the banks compete with each other to offer attractive rates, 12 months and one day later the chances are these ISAs will revert to far more miserly rates.

Banks rely on us leaving our money in their hands when the rates fall, or, more precisely, they rely on us not noticing when they cut rates. Just because a bank has a new market-leading savings account you cannot expect it to lead the market across the board. If you're operating an older account you're likely to be subsidising the new super rate that they are offering to new customers.

So many savings accounts offer teaser rates to attract customers and then lower rates that the Financial Conduct Authority is to investigate the savings market. In September 2013 it was estimated there was £400 billion in savings accounts paying less than 1% interest.

Check what you're getting on your money and before you congratulate yourself for getting 3% on your savings remember the inflation rate and also check if you're paying interest on any short-term loans such as credit cards or agreed overdrafts.

While it's good to have some ready cash available for an emergency and as part of your longer-term planning – something we deal with later in this book – you should consider using some savings to pay off overdrafts, credit cards and store cards which are attracting far, far higher interest rates than your cash on deposit can earn in the current climate.

When checking out savings accounts look for ones that reward regular saving if your intention is to put aside a set amount every month. Some pay a bonus if the money remains untouched for a set period. If you are able to tie up a lump sum for a year or more there are accounts that attract higher interest rates, but if you need the money early there will be a penalty of lost interest. Before you invest, work out what you might need the money for.

If you tie your money up for a set period or sign up for a savings account with an introductory bonus rate, make a note in your diary to check what the rate defaults to, or to move your account again once the anniversary is up.

DON'T PUT ALL YOUR EGGS IN ONE BASKET

While no savers have lost money in UK bank or building society savings accounts due to the default of these institutions in living memory, it's important not to exceed the limit for the UK compensation scheme. At the time of writing this is £85,000 per person per bank.

You have to be careful because of the mergers of banks and building societies in recent years. For example, Halifax, Birmingham Midshires and Bank of Scotland count as just one institution under the compensation scheme. The system isn't easy to fathom unless you know which bank bought which building society over the last 20 years, so check with the banks or building societies where you have savings to find out whether they count as separate institutions under the compensation scheme. They should have details in each branch, but these may not be easy to find. You can also check online.

DEBIT, CREDIT AND STORE CARDS

While bank base rates are at an all-time low, interest rates on credit and store cards are still exploitatively high. Credit cards have never been a cheap form of borrowing but the gap between the bank base rate and the amount we are charged has never been higher. Store cards can be even more expensive. The best way to fight back is to stop using these cards. If you cannot afford to pay them off in full each month you're only going to get further in debt.

Every week we receive tempting offers to take out new cards. The letters tell us that we have credit allocated to us and we can even transfer existing credit card debts and pay no interest for a year or more. Then we go shopping and it seems every shop wants us to have their store card. They offer an instant discount on the shopping you do that day and fail to mention the extortionate interest rate they will charge. Avoid. And if you already have a store card with a hefty debt now is the time to pay it off. Start with the highest interest rates first.

Only use a credit card to get cash in a dire emergency. Should you make the mistake of withdrawing cash from a machine using your credit card there's usually a fee attached.

Watch out for extra fees when paying with plastic. The cost of booking fees for using credit cards to buy plane, theatre, cinema or rail tickets can be hefty, even though regulations state that these should reflect the true cost to the company. The fees often don't show up until you have gone through the order process and are about to confirm the order, even though the extra cost should be revealed upfront. A Money Fight Club member – on noticing firms breaching the guidelines in these areas – would write to the firm to let them know they can't get away with it. A letter to the Office of Fair Trading may help stop the practice. The OFT's consumer credit responsibilities will be taken over by the Financial Conduct Authority during 2014.

❝ TOO MANY CHECKS CAST A SHADOW OVER YOUR CREDIT SCORE. ❞

Many cards entice you in by not charging interest on balance transfers from another card. This can be tempting if your credit card balance is beginning to look a little vertiginous and the interest is beginning to pile up, but moving a debt doesn't change your spending patterns.

New spending will attract interest and it's easy to get further into debt. On top of this, when you move cards – or take out a new one – the cardholder will carry out a credit reference check. Too many checks cast a shadow over your credit score. The best thing to do if transferring a debt across to a new card is to set up a standing order to pay a fixed amount each month so that the debt is cleared during the free period.

Here are some other top tips:

- **Don't forget to pay something off your card each month** – even if times are super tough. Failing to pay the minimum each month will incur a penalty, as well as the interest that has accrued. You will also get a black mark on your credit record that will take several years to be removed.

- **Pay off in full if you can.** Paying the minimum on your card each month will see the debt increase, even if you don't spend anything. Banks love customers who pay off the minimum each month as they end up paying many times the amount they borrowed over a period of many years.

- **Use credit and debit cards sparingly abroad.** The exchange rates can be even poorer than you get when you change cash at a bureau and they are not revealed until you get home and get your bill. There will also be additional fees levied by your own bank and possibly the foreign banks for getting cash or using a credit card. Most debit cards now levy costs for using them abroad so if you travel often, check out what charges are levied when you're choosing a bank account.

LOANS

It's funny how when we're saving money interest rates seem so low, but when we borrow the interest rates take your breath away.

Anyone needing a loan nowadays needs to compare interest rates very, very carefully. Only take out a long-term loan if you know you're not going to pay it off early. The banks claim the administrative costs for setting up loans are enormous and if you pay off early you will still have to pay these, so you won't save anything like the amount you expect.

Loans are also available from the finance companies run by supermarkets and other store groups, often in association with the high street banks. They advertise cheap rates but you need to read the terms and conditions carefully. The rate advertised is often the cheapest available and it's rarely given to people who really need to borrow, but is limited to those with the best incomes and credit records.

Before you take out a bank loan find out if you can get the money elsewhere. Some employers offer interest-free loans for transport season tickets or even for other purposes. Check if you qualify. Some insurance policies allow you to borrow at low interest rates – especially those taken out a long time ago.

If you need a large loan and you have a small mortgage you may be able to take out a further loan secured on your home. This would put your home at risk but the interest rates are often half as much as those on traditional bank loans that are not secured on property.

PAYDAY LOANS

Payday loan companies are now on almost every high street and advertise their *instant* loans on television and online. Their marketing campaigns are often humorous and friendly. They seem the answer to any short-term money problems and the emphasis seems to be on lending money quickly.

Payday loans should be avoided at all costs!

Money Fight Club members would like to see payday loans eradicated. The lenders never suffer and the interest rates they charge can work out annually at 4000% – or more! The borrower who fails to pay back on time is offered a new loan to help them out by rolling over the interest. Before the customer has time to pay back the original £100 loan it can become £500 and they've no chance of paying it back.

Even worse than this, because the loans are made

> **❝ THE FCA IS PLANNING NEW REGULATIONS TO CONTROL PAYDAY LOAN COMPANIES BUT AT THE TIME OF WRITING THERE IS NO DATE FOR THEIR IMPLEMENTATION. ❞**

instantly they've often been used by fraudsters who take out loans using other people's identities and withdraw the cash from an ATM. Often the victim first learns about the loan when monthly repayments are taken from their bank account.

In 2013 Citizens Advice carried out a survey of payday loan customers. They analysed 2000 of these loans from more than 100 lenders and found that in nine out of ten cases the borrowers were not asked to show that they could afford the repayments.

Margaret Hodge, the chairman of the Commons Public Accounts Committee said:

> "Some of these lenders use predatory techniques to target vulnerable people on low incomes, encouraging them to take out loans which, when rolled over with extra interest, rapidly become out-of-control debts. Such disgraceful practices by the shabby end of the credit market are costing borrowers an estimated £450m or more each year."

Payday lenders are licensed by the Office of Fair Trading but at the time of writing it had not fined any of the companies and had only revoked a few licences. As we went to press the OFT announced that it had referred payday lenders to the Competition Commission because of "deep-rooted problems with the way competition works."

Avoid payday loans under all circumstances. They can be as addictive as a drug; try them once and the temptation is to go back for more and go back more often. Things go wrong – unexpected bills, a cut in overtime hours, job loss – and only the payday loan companies benefit when they do.

You cannot defeat these dirty fighters, but if you know of cases when friends or relatives have been misled into deep debt tell the Financial Conduct Authority, which will be taking over from the Office of Fair Trading by the time you read this. The bad guys win when we keep quiet.

The FCA is planning new regulations to control payday loan companies but at the time of writing there is no date for their implementation.

CREDIT UNIONS

There can be financial help much closer to home and from people you know and trust. Credit unions are financial cooperatives that operate locally and offer small loans to members. There are some 500 credit unions in the UK and they have around 1m members. They all serve a particular community. It can be a town, an estate, a church, a union, an association or an employer. You can find your local credit union by contacting the Association of British Credit Unions Ltd, Abcul, on 0800 015 3060 or on **www.abcul.org** under 'Find Your Credit Union'.

The Archbishop of Canterbury announced in July 2013 that he wanted the church to support these institutions and provide stronger competition to payday lenders (although he was somewhat embarrassed to then discover the Church of England's own pension fund had money invested through a company which helped finance one payday lender – such is the tangled nature of modern money).

> **THE BAD GUYS WIN WHEN WE KEEP QUIET.**

The savers in a credit union fund all the loans that it makes – very much like building societies in the old days. You have to be a member to take out a loan and this usually costs a few pounds, but most unions do not require borrowers to be long-term savers.

Credit unions tend to lend between £50 and £3000 and charge annual rates of 6% to 26%. From April 2014 credit unions will be able to charge 3% a month on loans. While the latter seems high there are no hidden charges and it is a great deal cheaper than doorstep lenders or payday loan companies. The loans are not intended for people who can borrow easily from a bank or other commercial organisation.

Savers are likely to earn comparative rates to those offered by bank savings accounts and their savings are covered by the Financial Services Compensation Scheme. There is currently a £10,000 limit on the amount that can be saved with credit unions, but the government has been asked to increase this limit and is injecting money to modernise and expand them. The April 2014 increase to the interest rate they can charge is a move designed to make them more sustainable.

Some credit unions now offer pre-paid cards so that you can shop without risking getting into debt. Unions also offer help with budgeting and a few have current accounts and offer mortgages; the emphasis is on ensuring borrowers can afford their loans and are in control.

The credit union movement in the UK is relatively small compared to elsewhere, including America. You can't help wondering if that's partly because they offer honest loans without all the hype and promise of the big loan institutions with their massive advertising budgets and impressive offices.

According to a 2012 government-commissioned study into credit unions, some 7m of us use high-cost credit when credit unions could offer a cheaper alternative. While their membership is tiny currently compared to people borrowing from big lenders, it is starting to grow.

BORROWING OR SAVING – DON'T BE GRATEFUL

Our status increasingly seems to be based on a complex array of accessories – our salary, our job, the car we drive, the size and type of house we live in, our taste in food and wine, even where and how often we holiday.

This status is the result of numerous transactions – what we are paid and whether that's more or less than our outgoings; the size of our mortgage and the limit on our credit card(s). In some cases we may balance these transactions carefully, so that what comes in and what goes out match, or even allows us to save. In other cases there is a discrepancy between what we can afford and what we spend; how we want to be perceived and what we are worth in plain pounds and pennies.

Is it any wonder that what we earn, how much we save and what we owe (or can borrow) can profoundly influence how we feel about ourselves?

Here at Money Fight Club we think that one less positive outcome of this set up is that too many of us are too grateful to financial institutions that enable us. They provide the tools we need – bank accounts, credit cards, mortgages – and so they tend to get our gratitude.

But they don't deserve it. Most large financial institutions have behaved anywhere from poorly to appallingly in recent years and run up huge debts of their own. They only survive because we use them. Their status is entirely dependent on us – how many customers they have, their share of the mortgage market, etc.

Don't be grateful. Whether you're borrowing or saving, give yourself some respect for juggling all the financial tools at your disposal. As a good money fighter, don't weaken your position by getting into too much debt, or tying yourself into poor interest rates, or allowing a bank to convince you something is free when it's actually a mishmash of fees, charges and extras you don't need. Instead, sharpen your wits and find yourself something better.

ROUND 4

DEFENDING YOUR HOME

"This is my house, I have to defend it."

KEVIN MCCALLISTER (MACAULAY CULKIN), HOME ALONE

Your home may be your castle or your bedsit. You may be renting or buying. It may be your first step on the property ladder or the place where you plan to spend your twilight years. You may also have a second home, for rent or as a holiday hideaway. The most important thing is it's yours. Bricks and mortar may look pretty secure but there are numerous ways that paying for your home can pull the rug out from under your finances. Pay attention and put your fists up.

Decisions around where we live are some of the most emotionally charged and when emotions run high we often fail to pay attention to the practicalities. Moving house is one of the most stressful things we do and it's getting worse. Mortgages can be hard to secure, particularly if you're not that well paid or just starting on the property ladder and rents are rising fast. Then there are a load of scams and cons to trip you up too.

You need to get into serious training whether you want to buy or to rent.

Accommodation agencies, estate agents, banks, insurance companies, sellers and landlords can all make us feel vulnerable because they control our access to a home. So before you start to look at the property pages online or in your local paper you need to make sure you're up for the fight ahead.

We're often unfit to make these decisions. Research published by the Royal Institution of Chartered Surveyors (RICS) in spring 2013 revealed "common misconceptions and lack of understanding amongst consumers." Some 10% mistakenly believed estate agents act for the buyer, whilst nearly 20% wrongly thought they act equally for the buyer and seller. Nearly a third of first-time buyers admitted they did not have a good understanding of the purchase process. Yet buying and selling a home is the largest single financial transaction most of us will ever make.

Home ownership has rocketed since the 1950s, although this rise has been hit by the economic doldrums over the last few years. In the last decade or so renting has enjoyed a resurgence as many people find themselves priced out of ownership and the ability to secure a mortgage, or hit by the most recent recession. So whether you're looking to rent or buy – this is the Round for you.

BUYING AND SELLING PROPERTY

Is this your first time?

It may not seem like it at the time, but buying your first house is the easiest property purchase you will ever make because you don't have to sell at the same time. Conversely, the first time you sell can seem very complicated (and stressful) because you're now handling buying and selling transactions simultaneously.

First-time buyers tend to have sellers, estate agents and builders eager to gain their attention as there's no chain at the buyer's end that will stop the sale at the last minute.

Yet there are plenty of people who are out to make things as difficult as possible for everyone. Banks and mortgage lenders are probably the least helpful. They've been tasked by the government with lending more to home buyers but have managed to make the rules for borrowing so tough that it seems impossible for many to get a mortgage even when they can afford the payments.

More mortgages are being granted as a result of the Funding for Lending scheme that gives banks and other lenders access to cheap cash to fuel their lending and so boost the economy, but the three and a half year high in home mortgage approvals reported in the summer of 2013 was still a long way short of a normal mortgage market (the Bank of England reported 58,000 loans were approved in May 2013, against an historic average of 85,000). The Help to Buy scheme has also increased the number of buyers.

> **LOYALTY COUNTS FOR NOTHING THESE DAYS.**

If you're selling a property and moving on to another, what are you planning to do about your mortgage? If you're showing a profit there can be a temptation to release some of the equity, but take care. A holiday may sound like a wonderful idea but what you're actually doing is taking capital and using it like it was income.

If you've always managed to pay your mortgage on time that should put you in a stronger position when it comes to securing a new loan but don't expect lenders to be falling all over you. If it's a while since you moved you may be surprised how the market has changed. Your existing lender is a good place to start but don't assume that your track record will automatically secure you a good deal. Money Fight Club members know that loyalty counts for nothing these days.

First, let's have a look at some of the home ownership incentives that are on offer in England (you can find different schemes in Ireland and Scotland).

HOME OWNERSHIP INCENTIVES

There are now a variety of home ownership initiatives on the market. The traditional shared ownership scheme was set up by the government to help those who could not afford to buy their homes outright and there are newer initiatives – including the government-backed FirstBuy scheme – where the emphasis is on boosting your buying power or helping with the deposit. It's important to understand the differences:

- **Shared ownership scheme** – you buy between 25% and 75% of your home through a housing association and pay rent on the rest. This is also called the 'part buy part rent' scheme.

- **Shared equity schemes or equity loans** – you buy and own the whole property but there is a loan to bridge the difference between your deposit and the mortgage. Builders may offer this option. You put down a deposit, typically 5%, and take out a loan for another 85-90% of the price. The builder arranges a loan for the rest. You pay the loan back when you sell.

- **Shared ownership schemes for older people or those with disabilities** – for the older people scheme you need to be over 55. 'Home Ownership for People with Long-Term Disabilities' (HOLD) can help you buy if the properties available in the other HomeBuy schemes don't meet your needs.

- **FirstBuy** – government scheme to help first timers buy a new home which has now been replaced by Help to Buy.

- **NewBuy** – don't confuse FirstBuy with NewBuy, which was launched to stimulate the new build market. For NewBuy you don't have to be a first-time buyer and there's no limit on your level of income. The scheme lets you buy a newly built home with a deposit of only 5% of the purchase price (maximum £500,000).

- **Help to Buy** – the Help to Buy scheme from the government was rolled out in two phases. The first phase, launched in the 2013 Budget, was an extension of the FirstBuy scheme. You need a 5% deposit and a mortgage of up to 75%. The government provides a loan for the difference. It's available on new build homes up to £600,000.

- **Help to Buy Part Two** – the second part of Help to Buy started in October 2013, under which the government will offer a guarantee facility to lenders, backing mortgages of between 80% and 95% on any properties worth up to £600,000.

Don't assume that just because a scheme is government-backed it's automatically a good deal. We aren't that impressed with the deals and interest rates being offered under Help to Buy II. Check what else is out there even if it means that without the government backing you'll only be able to put up a smaller deposit.

There is also a trick that is used where some new build prices are quoted after the government subsidy is deducted, making them look better value than they actually are. The mortgages may be quoted over 35 years and the payments are on 80% of the property price. Also check out exactly what happens when you sell, how and exactly when any loan will need to be paid back, and how much of any profit increase in value you will be entitled to (and any costs that will be taken out of this). It will be a while before we start to hear of any bad experiences when it comes to selling. We'll monitor the situation and report back on our website **www.moneyfightclub.com**.

BUYING A NEW PROPERTY

New homes come with a guarantee that covers any major work being needed in the first ten years but, generally, new property prices are higher. It's also worth doing some research into the developer and taking a look at previous developments that are now a few years old. How are they holding up to the test of time and what are the resale values like?

The chance to choose some of the finishes and the brand new kitchen can look enticing but you're paying for these things one way or another. For those buying their first home it may be an advantage to start with carpets, a cooker, washing machine, dishwasher and maybe a built in fridge-freezer, but for those moving up the housing ladder they may already have kitchen appliances that they want to keep. Sometimes builders will offer a range of deals and enticements including taking your existing property off your hands. Don't be dazzled.

Like new cars, new properties lose value as soon as you move in and if they are in areas where property prices are not rising overall then it might be risky to buy if you don't plan to stay in the property for very long. It can be particularly hard to call the property market when your new house is part of a much bigger new development where nobody is entirely sure how the area will develop and how in-demand it will be.

Buyers also have to be careful because some property developers have made costs seem cheap by quoting 35-year mortgages, rather than for 25 years. They may also refuse to work with independent brokers and may restrict which properties they will offer shared-ownership or Help to Buy on.

GETTING A MORTGAGE
MAKING YOURSELF ATTRACTIVE TO LENDERS

As well as understanding the mortgage deals on offer, all home buyers, at every stage of their home-owning career, need to make themselves as attractive as possible to lenders before they even look at a property. It's not just a question of how much you can afford to borrow but it's also about securing the most attractive deals.

It doesn't matter if you can afford the repayments – the slightest transgression with a bank account, credit card, rent or loan could make it very hard to get a mortgage in today's market and certainly will make it tough to secure some of the better deals on offer. The lenders can be super-picky.

PRODUCING A BUDGET

First of all, to stand a chance in the ring with your bank manager you need to know where all your money goes. If you don't know that, you can't persuade him or her that you can afford a mortgage. Get your bank statements and credit card bills and make sure you have a clear record of where your cash goes.

How much do you earn? What is left after tax, national insurance and pension payments? If your monthly pay varies because of overtime, work out the average over the past year. This is your starting point.

The next stage is to find out where the money goes:

- If you have been saving regularly that's useful information and a print-out of your savings account or pass book is useful.
- If you're paying rent – even if it's to your parents – this should be accounted for.
- Those with an existing mortgage should sort out the paperwork.
- Take into account costs for travel to work and any other transport expenses.
- Food, heating, council tax, water rates.
- Loan payments (including student loan payments that are or may become due).
- Nights out, holidays and clothes.

All the above need to be noted down and you need to have evidence to back your story (receipts, etc.). Is your rent paid from your bank account every month? Do you pay your credit card off in full every month?

You need an easy-to-understand one-page version of what money comes in and where it goes. Don't just write it down – memorise it! Some lenders have had great fun of late with the type of questions they've asked borrowers. They say they need to know if you're a risk or not but the sort of questions can be downright intrusive, such as asking how much you spend at the hairdressers, on your lunches at work, or on driving lessons.

If you have a business-like budget with supporting evidence in the form of annotated bank statements, credit card bills, gas and electricity bills, etc., you will be well on the way to winning the bout.

CHECK YOUR CREDIT RECORD

Before you go toe to toe with a lender or your bank manager you need to check out what is in the public domain about your financial reliability. Carrying out a credit check costs a couple of quid and everyone should do it regularly to make sure there are no problems or mistakes.

Money Fight Club members know that even if they have a squeaky clean financial profile, financial institutions can stuff up royally on occasions. According to a 2010 survey carried out by consumer organisation Which?, one-in-eight of their members found their credit reports contained an error when they checked. The credit reference agencies told Which? that mistakes can arise for a number of reasons, including erroneous data supplied by your previous lenders or financial institutions.

The two main credit reference agencies – Experian and Equifax – offer an online service. Go to **www.experian.co.uk** or **www.equifax.co.uk** and they will provide a record of your recent credit history within seven working days. When the document arrives check it thoroughly.

There may be items on your record that look worse than they really are and can be fully explained. If a fraudulent purchase was added to your credit card and you disputed it and did not pay, it may appear as a failure to pay your credit card and leave an apparent black mark against you. Or if you moved out of a flat and the final gas bill for 12p never reached you and was not paid that will also leave a mark. Debts of a few pence frequently crop up and cause difficulties. Get rid of them.

If there are any black marks you need to contact the credit reference agency and ask it to add a brief explanation to their records. If there's incorrect information you can ask for it to be removed. Whatever you find, at least you're forewarned before you contact a lender and won't get caught off-guard. If your explanation is plausible and provable then you should be on your way to winning round one on points.

TOO SQUEAKY CLEAN?

Daft as it sounds you need a credit history to prove you're worth lending to. So if you've never had a loan or credit card it would actually help you if you applied for a credit card, used it to make purchases and paid it off in full each month. This turns you into a known quantity – somebody who pays off what they owe. The earlier you start this process the better your credit record when you apply for a mortgage.

You should also make sure you're on the Electoral Register for your current address. It stops lenders thinking you're an imposter.

WORK OUT WHAT YOU SHOULD BE ABLE TO BORROW

Don't leave it to the lenders to do the maths. If you have your budget under control and know roughly what you can borrow then you're on the way to victory. Take the high ground and work out what you may be good for. Generally four times the main salary or 3.5 times joint salaries for a couple are the borrowing levels that lenders are comfortable with, but there are exceptions and the main wage earner might be able to borrow five terms earnings. It will depend on the lender and the circumstances, which include the size of your deposit.

You can find out online what the general rules are for the different lenders and there are plenty of mortgage calculator systems online too. These will give you an idea of what you should be able to borrow. If you're a long way short of the price of the properties you're interested in you may still be able to get a loan but you will need a guarantor in the form of a close relative who has savings they can deposit to guarantee your payments.

That said, a good money fighter knows when to walk away. It's not just about what you can borrow but what you personally can afford.

CHEAP MORTGAGES - THE DEVIL'S IN THE DETAIL

The lenders shout loud about their best-ever fixed-rate mortgage deals at 1.99%, but somehow don't seem to lend to that many homebuyers at these cheap rates. When they do there can be huge arrangement fees – up to £1995 – which make the loans poorer value, especially for smaller fixed rate mortgages over two years. So if you're buying at the bottom end of the market and could end up moving on relatively quickly – as first-time buyers so often do – beware.

That isn't all. The best mortgage deals are reserved for those with the biggest deposits, so while someone with a 40% deposit may be able to get a loan at 1.99%, those with a 5% to 10% deposit are likely to pay more than twice as much.

FIXED VS. VARIABLE-RATE DEALS

Some fixed-rate deals (where the interest is fixed at a certain percentage for a set period of time) are higher than the standard variable rates (where the interest rate can change) offered by lenders. The bank base rate was fixed at 0.5% in March 2009, had remained unchanged into autumn 2013 and is not expected to increase before 2016, but lenders want to be protected if the rates do go up, hence why fixed rates are so high.

Fixed-rate mortgages are popular because they give certainty about mortgage payments for a fixed amount of time. Your payments cannot increase for the two, three or five years of the fix, but you also need to look into what happens when it finishes, especially for two-year fixes.

Usually the mortgage moves straight on to the lender's standard variable rate at the end of the fixed-rate period. Surprisingly (or not) often the lenders that have the best fixes also have higher than usual standard variable mortgage rates. In other words, the cheap fix lures borrowers in and then the buyers are charged more than the market average for most of the term of the mortgage. Some lenders offer a further fix to borrowers when the first one finishes, but these are unlikely to be as good value as the rates being offered to lure in new borrowers.

To win the house-buying battle you need to develop a view on what the interest rate will be when the fix finishes and what the total cost of the mortgage will be when arrangement fees are included. Over 25 years that £1999 could grow to £5000+. Taking a view on interest rates isn't as complicated as you might think. The key is not to take one opinion as gospel – and certainly not the opinion of the person selling you the mortgage. Read the papers, listen to the news and do a little internet research.

> **WORK OUT IF YOU CAN AFFORD THE REPAYMENTS IF THEY GO UP.**

You also need to need to know exactly what your mortgage payments will be from the outset. Interest rates are one thing – pound signs are quite another. Can you afford them, comfortably, especially when you have other bills to pay? If you're a first time or relatively novice buyer what is liable to change in your circumstances? For example, have you plans to marry or start a family? Get your advisor or mortgage provider to do some of the work for you. For example, what will mortgage repayments be at the end of the fixed period? What would they be if opting for a standard variable rate and interest rates increase by one percentage point? Work out if you can afford the repayments if they go up.

With standard variable rates lenders used only to change the rate when the bank base rate increased or fell. Now, lenders feel able to change their rates at whim – in 2012 some of the biggest mortgage lenders decided to increase their mortgage rates for millions of customers without bank base rates increasing. Exercise care and make sure to shop around for the best variable rate as you come to the end of fixed-rate mortgage periods.

TRACKER MORTGAGES

With tracker mortgages you are charged a fixed amount above the bank base rate for the entire mortgage term. They've proved a good deal in recent years because before the 2007/8 financial crisis there was no expectation that the official bank base rate would fall to 0.5%.

For thousands of home buyers this apparent tie in to the base rate was broken in 2013 when the Bank of Ireland decided that even though the base rate had been unchanged for more than four years, they would unilaterally increase the payments for their tracker customers. Customers who believed they had signed up for a mortgage that was base rate plus 1.75% until the end of the mortgage found that it increased to base rate plus 2.49% from May 2013 and then to base plus 3.99% from October 2013. Those who had a buy-to-let mortgage found their loans increase from base rate plus 1.75% to base rate plus 4.49% in May 2013.

The mortgages had 'life' or 'lifetime' in their names but the bank decided that it could not afford to honour the contracts because it had to maintain greater levels of capital. This was a significant change in market conditions. The bank sought refuge in itty bitty fine print in the contract and increased payments with just a couple of months' notice. Death and taxes may be certain. Mortgage repayments less so.

At the time of writing in 2013 one more lender had increased its tracker rates for buy-to-let mortgages and it seemed likely that other banks would sneak similar clauses into the small print of their tracker-loans or even their fixed-rate mortgages. So whatever the salesman says about how the mortgage will work and whatever it's called you need to check the full details and what the worst case-scenario would be.

FLEXIBLE OR OFFSET MORTGAGES

Flexible or offset mortgages allow people to link a savings account and a mortgage account with the same lender so the savings in the first cancel out the equivalent amount of loan in the latter. Home buyers may not be able to use savings as part of the deposit when they buy a home because they're expecting tax bills or other expenses in the future, but while they have savings they can reduce their mortgage payments with a flexible or offset mortgage.

Some of these loans also allow borrowers to take back money they've already paid off their mortgage if they need it for other projects. In this way someone who has a flexible mortgage can make payments for a couple of years and then decide to use a mortgage reserve or drawdown facility to get cash up to a pre-set limit. These loans give access to money at the standard variable mortgage rate instead of the person having to take out a separate loan or overdraft. Once again, banks offering these deals can change the terms and arbitrarily reduce the amount that can be borrowed. Always leave yourself some slack.

INTEREST-ONLY LOANS

In general, interest-only loans are the equivalent of renting a property long term but having to pay for all the maintenance along the way.

There are currently more than a million homeowners who are at risk of losing their homes because they were sold interest-only mortgages and have no means of paying off the loans at the end of the 20 or 25-year term. In some cases the interest-only loans were sold alongside an investment product such as an endowment mortgage (a mortgage designed to be paid off using an insurance policy). Endowment mortgages have dramatically underperformed.

In many cases people have been sold the loans on the expectation that property prices would increase significantly and selling the property would allow them to realise a tidy profit, pay off the loan and have enough for another (if less expensive) property purchase. However, in large parts of the country house prices have fallen, putting many homebuyers in negative equity 'where their loans are larger than the value of the property'. These interest-only loans should no longer be on offer to private buyers but it's possible that salesmen and brokers may put them forward as a way of getting on to the housing market.

Interest-only mortgages can be marketed as buy-to-let loans, as these require a lower income on the basis that the borrower is going to get rental income to pay the loan. Buy-to-let loans now account for around 14% of mortgages and these loans are not covered by the Financial Ombudsman service as buy-to-let borrowers are seen as small businesses. So if the lender decides to increase the mortgage payments arbitrarily there's little that the borrowers can do.

THE KEY PLAYERS (AT LEAST ONE OF THEM IS YOU)
THE BUYER

The smart buyer doesn't take anything at face value. Lots of sellers lie by their actions or words. Many will repeatedly paint over a damp patch to disguise it from buyers. They will tell a buyer what a wonderful home it has been and how they are selling reluctantly. They won't tell them that the property has been on the market for six months and that they are increasingly desperate to get any offer because of the traffic noise during the rush hour or the difficulty of finding anywhere to park.

When you're buying you need to act cool. The first time you view a property you may have rose-tinted glasses on so go back and take a long, hard look around. Also check out the property at different times of the day.

Whatever you may read about the market, there are still lots of properties for sale and buyers should still have the winning hand in all except a few small areas. The first house or flat you like may be taken off the market because another buyer has offered more, but nothing is lost until the contracts are exchanged.

THE SELLER

The savvy seller is realistic. They remember that the housing market has been dodgy for several years and there are millions of people trapped in homes they cannot sell for one reason or another. They may be in debt or just desperate for an extra bedroom or two to house their growing families.

If you're selling remember to keep calm. If you look and act desperate both the estate agent and any buyer will pick up on that. When potential buyers are viewing your property for sale, their sighs of boredom and laughable first offer may be bluffs designed to rattle your cage. Your buyer may also swear blind they're no longer looking but don't count your chickens until exchange takes place. The survey may also upset things. A buyer may well want to negotiate the price down and turn a small damp patch into a major issue. Remember not to get too excited about the first offer you receive – no matter what your agent may tell you..

It isn't just about price. A first-time buyer with a mortgage arranged and nothing to sell, who needs to get out of their rented property in the near future, could be a better prospect for you to sell to than a second-time buyer who has not yet exchanged contracts on the sale of their current home.

THE MORTGAGE BROKER

If you're self-employed – even if you have three years of audited accounts – or have any special circumstances that need explaining, then it may pay to have a mortgage broker in your corner. In days of old some brokers would bend the rules to get loans for people with shaky backgrounds but things have changed. That said, check them out and ideally go with recommendations from somebody you trust who has used the broker in the past. If you have a financial advisor, they may recommend brokers they've worked with in the past.

Be honest and if there's something in your past that may make getting a mortgage difficult and your mortgage broker seems to gloss over this, ask yourself why. A mortgage broker will charge a fee, but this should be explained at the outset so you can decide if you can afford it and whether it's worth having someone in your corner.

ESTATE AGENTS

Estate agents work for the property seller but it's sometimes easy to get confused. If you're buying, be sceptical about what the agent tells you about the keenness of the asking price and the desirability of location. Drive around the area to see what it is like and how many For Sale boards there are. If you're selling do your own research about the market and achievable prices. Websites like **www.rightmove.co.uk**, **www.zoopla.co.uk** and **www.landregistry.gov.uk** have made this very easy.

VALUERS/SURVEYORS

Even if your budget is tight it's important to pay for an inspection of the property you want to buy. All being well this service will find any damp, subsidence or potential flooding problems. If you're selling, it's worth engaging with the valuer as they walk round your property. If nothing else you might get a heads up on any issues. As a buyer, shop around and seek recommendations when selecting a valuer.

A valuer may be appointed by your mortgage company but don't just assume everything is out of your hands. They are providing a cursory report for the lender and are not working for you. You need to appoint your own valuer in addition to the one the lender uses. Make sure they work for you. Ask to speak to them on the phone and build a relationship. Let them know if there's anything you're particularly interested in.

Obviously you wouldn't want your mortgage provider to turn you down or offer you a smaller mortgage because there are problems, but wouldn't you rather know if there was something about the property that could affect its future value or cost you money to repair?

MAKING (AND RECEIVING) AN OFFER

Use the Rightmove, Zoopla and Land Registry sites to help you do your homework to make sure you don't pay too much (when buying) or settle too low (when selling).

Buyers have to be bold. Feel you can knock 10% off the price? This isn't an insult. It's a sighting shot. If the property has been on the market for a time then the seller is more likely to listen.

Property pages, local, national and online, produce statistics on what percentage of the asking price properties are typically sold for. Very rarely is the figure above 95%. In a lot of areas it's 92% or 93%. So if you view a property on sale for £250,000 it's worth putting in a first offer of £225,000 while detailing why you're a good buyer.

Sellers need to be steadfast. Don't be psyched into accepting too low a price but make it clear you welcome the opportunity to negotiate. Think about how you can make your circumstances, as well as your home, an attractive proposition. Flexibility on completion, buying a property with little or no chain, a willingness to negotiate on contents, etc., can sweeten the deal. No matter how much you need to sell, avoid giving off any whiff of desperation.

STAMP DUTY

Stamp duty is charged on the price you pay and the amount goes up in tiers:

- Properties up to £125,000 pay nothing.
- £125,000 to £250,000 the tax is 1%.
- £250,000 to £500,000 it's 3%.
- £500,000 and £1 million it's 4%.
- £1m to £2 million it's 5%.
- All properties above £2 million, the duty is 7%.

These rates are worth considering carefully. For example, if you buy just under £250,000 you will pay around £2495 in stamp duty but if you pay just above you incur more than £7500. As a seller, if your price is just over one tier but you're including items like freestanding fridges and cookers or other items of furniture (chattels), in the price, you may want to sell them separately to the purchaser to bring the total of the house sale into the tier below. Your solicitor can still handle this.

OTHER COSTS AND POSSIBLE PROBLEMS

You need to do your homework about potential difficulties with a property. It's too late when you have paid for a survey and a solicitor so you need to think ahead. The costs of buying and selling – stamp duty, solicitors, surveyors, estate agents, carpets and curtains – are now so high that you should ideally plan to live in a property for at least five years, probably longer.

In that time you might start a family, take up gardening or start a business, so it's worth finding out about schools, potential planning permission for an extension or whether there are covenants against a change of use. If nothing else, good schools, planning permission or flexibility of use will help you when you come to sell.

As a rule of thumb, if a property appears to be cheap there's a reason for it. It may be leasehold and the length of the lease is less than lenders want, or it may have defects that need correcting. Also check if there have been floods in the area recently. The extreme weather of the past couple of years has brought many more properties into flood risk.

Leasehold properties can be cheaper if the lease has less than 80 years left to run. Lenders don't like short leases but if you have a big deposit and plan to extend the lease then it may be a good deal. Leaseholders have a legal right to extend the lease with the cost increasing as the lease nears its end. For example, it will cost about £4000 to extend the lease by 50 years on a modest property with 80 years to run and a £50 ground rent (this ground rent is a regular payment leaseholders have to make to the landlord). The higher the ground rent and the shorter the lease the more you will pay. There's a formula for calculating this and estate agents should be able to provide the information.

BUYING A RETIREMENT PROPERTY

Those who are house-rich and nearing retirement may decide to downsize and may consider a property built specifically for retirees. These properties are usually leasehold and brand new. They offer large grounds tended by a gardener, restaurants and social activities with other residents. They look attractive but these should be approached with caution because there can be lots of problems.

First of all, the service charges can increase rapidly. You need to establish what the service charge covers and how it is calculated. If there is a residents' association you should be able to find out if there have been problems with service charges or poor repairs and maintenance.

Selling may also be difficult as there is a limited market and people like to buy these properties brand new rather than second hand. More importantly there will be restrictions on who you can sell to and there are likely to be charges for administering re-sales. These can be hefty and you may also be charged a contribution to the sinking fund for major repairs that may be needed in the future.

Before buying you need to see the Purchasers' Information Pack and it may be useful to consult the Age UK advice service at **www.ageuk.org.uk**. Also check out if the scheme manager is a member of the Association of Retirement Housing Managers at **www.arhm.org**.

While selling the family home and buying a retirement property may free up money for your family or make your retirement more comfortable it can store up problems for your family when they try to sell the property after your death and find that the value is much lower than when you bought, or they may struggle to sell at all.

DOWNSIZING

An alternative to a retirement property is to think about buying a property that will serve you better in old age. Useful features to look out for are: proximity to bus stops and railway stations, not far from friends and family, ground floor bathrooms (or room to install one), a flight of stairs that will make fitting a stair lift relatively easy, a small garden, etc.

RENTING

Rents are rising faster than incomes and house prices, particularly in London where it seems few under 30 can save enough to buy even the smallest flat. That said, Generation Rent still does not find it easy to find a home to rent. We will help you to get fighting fit for the task.

While landlords want to get the highest rents possible from their tenants, there are lots of other ways you can help yourself to punch above your weight.

First of all you need to build your profile as a reliable renter. To do this you need references, preferably from former landlords, mortgage lenders, employers, university accommodation managers, your church or a charity that you have volunteered for. Landlord or letting agency references are the most important because they have a record of you paying rent on time and the state you left their accommodation in.

First-time renters or those who have previously flat-shared won't have the preferred references but they may be able to get a letter from former housemates or demonstrate they are reliable by getting their HR department to provide evidence of how long they've worked for a company and how much they earn.

Landlords and agents want to be sure you can afford to rent a property and some will have strict rules on what you can rent on your salary. This may mean that the rent has to be less than a third of your take-home pay. If the rent is more they will want a guarantor. This may be a parent or other close relative who is a property owner and whose employer will provide evidence of their reliability.

Realistically if you want to rent a one or two bedroom property on one salary you're likely to fall short. Bank statements and proof that you lived in the same address for a year or more will help to reassure a letting agent. Sometimes an agent will ask those whose salary is less than ideal to pay several months of rent in advance or may double the deposit needed from one month's rent to two.

HOW MUCH RENT CAN YOU AFFORD?

Even if the landlord does not require the rent to be a certain minimum ratio of your salary, you need to know you can afford the property. As a rule of thumb the rent, gas, electricity, water and council tax should not be more than 50% of your take-home pay.

You need to sort out what's included in the rent first of all. If it's a flat or house-share this can be even more difficult. It's easier if you're a straightforward single tenant in that you're responsible for the council tax – unless it's a house in multiple-occupation or the landlord lives in the building. You also must budget for heating, electricity, water rates, TV licence, broadband and even satellite TV. You need an idea of what these bills will add up to before you move in.

Ask for the energy performance certificate of the property. This will indicate how expensive it will be to heat – an A grade is best. E, F and G grades suggest there isn't enough insulation, the heating system is poor or doors and windows are ill-fitting.

Remember, if you're sharing a property you're legally responsible if you're named on any bills. You may claim back your share from another tenant but if they move on without paying you will be responsible for the full bill.

LETTINGS AGENTS AND LANDLORDS

Find a reputable agent; one that's concerned about the landlords they represent. Good tenants want to rent from good landlords, who are represented by good agents. Trust your gut reaction; if you don't like the agent your tenancy will be more difficult.

Agents often want rapid turnover as these give more opportunities for them to charge fees to both parties. If an agent is willing to let to the first person to view a property they are likely to be just after the letting fee and any other fees they can charge, such as for taking your references, a finder's fee and an inventory fee. You should be wary of an agent like this. A good letting agent is concerned about keeping tenant and landlord happy by looking after both parties.

There are confidence tricksters who advertise non-existent accommodation and ask for an upfront fee to see the property and may charge a substantial deposit to several people, who all believe that they will be moving into a flat. Make sure any agent you deal with is a member of a professional organisation. The Association of Residential Letting Agents has a directory of its members available on its website: **www.arla.co.uk**. You can also check the National Association of Estate Agents website: **www.naea.co.uk**

Unlike agents, landlords like people who will rent for more than six months, as each new tenant involves costs for the landlord such as cleaning and decorating and every time a tenant leaves there's a risk that the property will be empty for several weeks or even months.

If you want to rent for a longer period see if you can talk directly to the landlord or make sure the agent passes this information on. A landlord may even reduce the rent for someone who wants a property for two years rather than six months. Good landlords will want to meet a prospective tenant before they move in because they figure that a good relationship will stop tenants from wrecking their property.

From your perspective, if you can form a good relationship with your landlord your rent may not be increased quite so often. Landlords don't generally like to lose good tenants and increasing the rent can encourage tenants to buy their own place or at least to move somewhere cheaper so that they can start saving seriously.

DEPOSITS

Before you can move into a rented property you quite often need a deposit equal to at least a month's rent plus the first month's rent. There may be extra charges as well, such as an agency fee of up to £600, another fee for references of up to £275 and a £200 renewal fee may be due when the lease is extended.

This is tough for people moving from another rental property because they are unlikely to get their original deposit back before they have to pay the new deposit. The deposit is to safeguard the landlord if the tenant fails to pay or damages the property. It has to be lodged in one of the official schemes – Deposit Protection Scheme, Tenancy Deposit Scheme, My Deposits or Capita Tenancy Deposit Protection – which should mean you will get it back eventually. Check that your landlord uses one of these schemes before you pay a deposit.

Usually the landlord or agent will organise an inventory of the property's contents and the condition of the furniture and property when you move in – often with photographic evidence – and then will do the same after you have left. If they find, for example, the furniture has been wrecked or the carpet badly stained then they will withhold part, or all, of the deposit to cover this. If you disagree with the amount withheld then the deposit scheme will mediate. For more details on deposits and other rights and responsibilities of tenants, see government advice at **www.gov.uk/private-renting**.

THE RENTAL CONTRACT

You should ask for a copy of your contract and take time to read it as this will tell you what your rights are as an assured short-hold tenant. Typically you're agreeing to be a tenant at the rent stated for six months (sometimes 12 months) and after that time you can give two months' notice or the landlord can give you two months' notice to leave or increase your rent. The document should give the date the tenancy starts, when rent should be paid, when it can be reviewed and what you would have to pay if you terminated the tenancy early. Landlords who don't supply a contract within 28 days when requested can be fined.

Tenants have the legal right to live in a property that's safe and in a good state of repair. If the landlord does not carry out repairs don't be tempted to stop paying your rent as you could be evicted. Instead, you need to get help from the local council or housing groups and should enlist the help of the agent.

You should allow access for repairs and should also be told what access the landlord or his/her agent wants to the property. Most will want to check on a regular basis that you're not wrecking the place and may want to undertake repairs or decoration. They should give you at least 24 hours written notice of these inspections or other visits.

The contract will also state whether you're allowed to sub-let the property or what type of tenancy it is if you're already sharing. For example, under a joint tenancy each of the tenants is responsible for the full rent. If you want to be only responsible for your share of the rent then you need two separate tenancies. Landlords may be averse to this because it would put them at risk if your flatmate moves out and not you.

SOCIAL HOUSING

Local councils and housing associations usually work on a combined housing list, which means that home seekers only need to make one application. To be eligible for social housing you need to be able to show that you're in housing need and over 18 years old. People with a local connection have an advantage but there isn't enough housing for all who need it so those with the greatest need are most likely to succeed.

You will need to complete an application form giving information about overcrowding and health issues. The council will then assess what priority band you're in. If you disagree with the decision you can ask for the band to be reviewed.

HOME INSURANCE

Everyone – buyers or renters – should have contents insurance to cover against theft, fire or accidental damage. The price varies according to where the property is and the value of your possessions. The level of security at the property will also influence the cost. You should have five lever locks on the entrance and exit doors whether you own the property or are renting it. You also need window locks.

If you're in a flat-share then the cover is more limited but there are specific policies available from about £60 a year. These often cover your possessions wherever you move to and are ideal for students and people in their first flat share or job. Use price comparison sites such as **www.moneysupermarket.com, www.moneysavingexpert.com** or specialist renting sites like **www.spareroom.co.uk** to find the best deal for your postcode. Make sure you read all the small print and understand what will not be covered by the policy.

As a renter you don't need to take out buildings insurance but the owners of property should have cover. If you have a mortgage you will be required to insure the building that you have a mortgage on. If there are problems you may need a specialist insurer but otherwise a price comparison site should be able to help.

THE WORD 'HOME' CLOUDS OUR JUDGMENT

Home is where the heart is, An Englishman's home is a castle, Home Sweet Home.

Whatever its size or value, our home takes up a huge amount of emotional headspace. A home doesn't just mean security, but is a symbol of our social standing. At different stages we want different things from our home. The flat share with its posters and dubious fridge contents is just as important to the young student as the palatial pile with Doric columns and his 'n' her garages for the couple looking to demonstrate how far they've come in their respective careers.

When it comes to finding and securing a new home, or relinquishing an old one, we have to reach an emotional detachment. By all means pay attention to your instincts – does this property feel right? – but don't let volatile emotions such as desire or dissatisfaction cloud your judgment.

For example, you may feel your home, with its quirky colours and charming knickknacks, is worthy of top dollar, but all potential buyers can see is garish clutter. While you firmly believe you deserve to rent a lovely riverside apartment, or buy the rose-covered country home of your dreams, the budget may not stack up. Estate agents, mortgage brokers and landlords can play you emotionally and pressure you into making a poor decision. You need to cool down and focus, whether you're renting or buying.

Sometimes the simple act of thinning out your personal possessions and repainting in neutral colours can bring about an emotional detachment and prepare you for a sale. As a buyer, try pretending that you're actually buying for someone else. Give yourself a little distance and objectivity.

When renting, don't get panicked into signing by agents' descriptions of the queues of people hot on your heels waiting to snap up this damp hovel. See not opting for a property as a choice – not a failure. If you're choosing a property as part of a group of sharers, plan your tactics in advance before you start viewing and don't show your hand. If people starting picking out which room they'd like or cooing over the retro Formica in the kitchen, the agent knows he's got you. Think poker face. Discuss your views after you leave, out of the agent's earshot.

Think strategically. What's the point of getting all hot under the collar because a prospective purchaser just told you the first thing they'd do is pull down the bookshelves you put up shortly after you moved in? This is a military campaign. If you've already decided to withdraw (sell) why go on the defensive?

Likewise, as a buyer, what exactly are you spending money on – their choice of bathroom tiles or the location, proximity to transport and schools, and the number of rooms? Think purpose not paint colour.

It's not a home until you move in. Make sure you buy value, rather than paying through the nose.

ROUND 5

TRAVEL

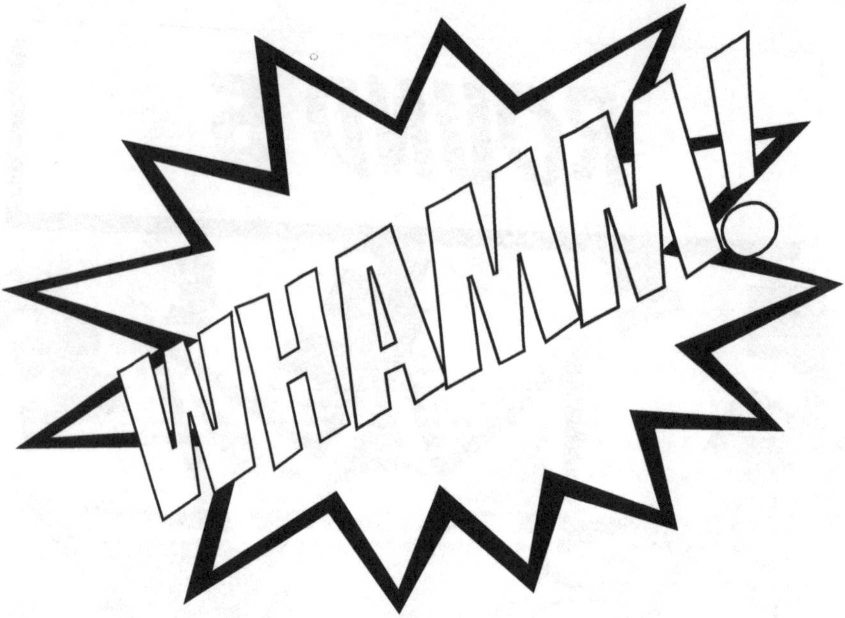
WHAMM!

"A journey of a thousand miles begins with a single step."

LAOZI, ANCIENT CHINESE PHILOSOPHER

Road, rail, bus, car... all travel comes with a cost and the cost is rising. In spring 2013 the AA claimed that spiralling fuel prices were forcing drivers off the road. Rail fares for season ticket holders increased by an average of 4.2% when the latest fares increase hit in January 2013.

Yet travel is short of a champion: when the Office of Fair Trading (OFT) carried out a study of the UK petrol and diesel market it decided that further regulation was not needed and that competition ensured garages didn't overcharge.

When the BBC commissioned a survey into UK travel costs back in 2007 they were higher than anywhere else in Europe. People in the UK spent 15% of disposable income on transport and double the amount on fares when compared with other Europeans. More recent figures from the TUC trade union organisation show that between 2008 and 2012 average rail fares increased by over 26%, while average wages rose by under 10% over the same period – well under the rate of inflation.

A survey by Asda Money in May 2013 indicated a third of parents travelled without travel insurance, saying they could not afford it. A month earlier a **sunshine.co.uk** survey revealed that of the trips abroad that never get beyond the planning stage, finance was cited as the reason in 42% of cases.

While we may have some control of when, where, how often and how much we spend going on holiday or enjoying leisure activities, we still need to get to work or get our children to school.

TRAVELLING TO WORK

For most of us, one of the biggest problems with travel to and from work is that employers want us all to arrive at (roughly) the same time. This means that train commuters often cannot get a seat but they pay much more than travellers at less busy times of the day. The roads are clogged and those going into central London are hit by the congestion charge.

Working different hours can save you a great deal. Everyone has the right to ask for flexible working hours but companies don't have to oblige with the concession. However, you may be able to put a good case for starting later and finishing later if this will extend the hours that your place of work is open for customers and clients.

Find out when off-peak travel applies to your journey. Rail and bus companies try to move passengers to times that are less busy by offering cheaper rates. Not only can you benefit from off-peak fares, on trains you can often get further discounts by using a 16-25 Railcard, a Senior Railcard or a Network Railcard. You pay £30 for a Railcard but off-peak fares are then 33% cheaper.

If you find you have to make a journey where the outward section has to be undertaken in peak time, it may make sense to buy two tickets – a peak outward fare and an off-peak return. Buying online in advance can also save you money. If you can research your journey in advance it's worth looking at different fare permutations and even travelling via different operators or by specific routes.

Even when you buy on the day at a ticket office it's worth saying "What is the cheapest ticket for..." rather than "Can I have a ticket for...". Some ticket office staff are surprisingly knowledgeable, particularly if you buy your ticket when they're not too busy. Could you pop down to the ticket office the day before, for example?

If you travel by car, travelling outside of rush hour can lead to less crawling along in jams and a steadier driving pace, which can improve your mileage. The London congestion charge can also be avoided if you can change your working hours and be parked before

7am and leave after 6pm. Some workers choose to do a four-day week to avoid the charge.

It's worth doing the research as it's possible to halve your travel costs by acting smart.

TRAINS

SEASON TICKETS

The average annual rail season ticket is around £2500 and every New Year it increases by more than inflation. In 2013 the average price per mile travelling by train with an annual season ticket was 16p and for monthly season tickets it was 18p. Due to the timing of the price increases, the best time to buy annual tickets is usually on 31 December. Check with your operator for specific details.

Annual season tickets can work out cheaper but don't just go by the figures given by your train operator. As with miles per gallon (MPG) on cars, these can be misleading, as nobody travels to work five days a week, 52 weeks a year. Do your own maths – at the very least deduct your holidays. If the weekly season ticket would be £96.50 and the annual season ticket is £3860 then those who have four weeks holiday a year will pay £80.41 a week – a saving of £16 a week – for their travel to work. This is not such a good deal for people who are teachers or college lecturers who travel to work fewer weeks a year.

> **IT'S WORTH DOING THE RESEARCH AS IT'S POSSIBLE TO HALVE YOUR TRAVEL COSTS BY ACTING SMART.**

Travelling off-peak can mean substantial savings. For example, a weekly season ticket in 2013 from Haywards Heath to London of £96.50 can come down to £13.40 a day, or £67 off-peak. If you have a Railcard this then comes down further to £8.95 a day and £44.75 – half the price of the weekly season ticket. If you don't need to work in the office every day then the savings can be more.

Paying for a season ticket with an overdraft or your usual credit card is likely to cut the savings dramatically because of interest rates, but there are ways of winning the travel cost battle. Plan ahead and apply for a credit card that gives you an interest-free period of a year or more for new purchases. So long as you make the monthly minimum payments you won't pay any interest on the loan.

It's also worth finding out if your employer offers interest-free season ticket loans. Lots of companies do but they may not advertise the benefit widely. Once again you need to plan ahead to have the cash at the right time. The money is then taken from your monthly pay.

If you have an annual, monthly or weekly season ticket, use it socially to get better value. The extra journeys are free in the evening or at weekends.

COMMUTING BY BUS

Transport for London bus fares are good value and routes extend out some ten miles from the centre. While they can take a little longer than the underground (assuming the tube service is running well), if you buy your fare with an Oyster card there's a flat pay-as-you-go fare on bus and tram travel, with no peak/off-peak difference. To take overland trains or underground can be many times the cost.

At the time of writing a peak time bus journey was £2.40, which reduced to £1.40 by using a pre-paid Oyster card. Using the tube is £4.50 in one zone or £2.10 with an Oyster card. The price increases the more zones you travel. You can also save on both bus and underground fares in London if you buy it as part of an off-peak travel card.

Other towns and cities offer similar schemes for regular travellers.

TRAINS

Travelling by train can be incredibly expensive if you don't do your research and plan ahead. The rail companies can charge pretty much what they like for unregulated train tickets, which account for about half of all journeys. If you just turn up at a station and ask for a ticket it can feel like being punched in the stomach, especially if you need to travel at specific times. Train companies advertise tempting fares from London to Scotland, Devon or Wales, etc., but these are not available to last-minute travellers.

Each company allows tickets to be bought 12 weeks ahead of travel and they have a limited number of very cheap offers (called advance fares) for those who buy online in advance. If you're planning a journey in good time, at least some rail companies allow you to set up a text or email alert so you're notified when the tickets become available. But if getting the best deal is important to you don't rely on the alert. Go online regularly as the 12-week window is approaching to see if the tickets are on sale yet.

Buying direct from the rail company you will be travelling with is often cheaper than buying tickets from organisations that sell them on behalf of all the rail companies, but whenever you're quoted a price it's best to compare other options and providers. Any rail company's website can sell you a ticket for a journey with any provider, but some (for example **www.eastcoast.co.uk** and **www.eastmidlandstrains.co.uk**) will offer you a discount if buying tickets for their train services direct from their website. East Coast also run a loyalty points scheme – sort of *train miles*. Another train travel loyalty scheme is run by train ticket purchase website **www.redspottedhanky.com**.

If your journey will involve two rail companies – it's worth checking whether it will be cheaper to book the journey in two separate pieces. For example, if travelling from Ipswich to Brighton via London with Greater Anglia and Southern, you should check whether it will be cheaper to buy two tickets – one from Ipswich to

London and a second from London to Brighton – rather than a single ticket for the full journey.

If you have to start in the rush hour it can make sense to split the journey into two fares, so that you pay for the first part of the journey as a peak journey and then buy an off-peak ticket for the part of the journey that takes place after the off-peak qualifying time. This might mean that you buy a ticket from, say, London Kings Cross to Stevenage and then pay for one from Stevenage to your destination in York. To qualify for this the train needs to stop at the station you 'split' your journey at, but you don't need to get off.

The cheapest trains will be the ones that no one else wants to travel on. These include very early trains in non-commuter areas, very late trains and very slow, stopping trains. It can cost twice as much to get a fast train from London to Birmingham as a slow stopping one. Consider how important speed is to your trip. If you take a good book and your own refreshments – train food and drink prices can be extortionate – there are good savings to be had.

There are also good deals if you're travelling off-peak with friends or family. The outward and return journey must be taken together but it's possible to get half price travel for all in the group. Check the website of the company you will be travelling with.

If your ticket limits you to one particular rail company, one route, or one specific train, you can't get on another one unless your booked train is cancelled or service is severely disrupted. If there's no announcement and your booked train is very late ask a guard or the station staff if you can get a different train.

PLANES

Only the super-rich commute by air, but most of us use air travel for holidays and once again the basic rules are the same: plan early, do your research, check the details and book early (unless you can afford to risk being able to bag a last minute deal because your plans are flexible). Travelling during the school holidays is a bit like being beaten up with both hands tied behind your back, but there are deals to be had if you're willing to put in the time online.

Cheap air fares are rarely as cheap as they first appear. The so-called no frills airlines have a lot of new tricks to try to part us from more money than we intended to pay and airlines seem to make it impossible for you to change your mind about when you're going to travel without it costing you more. Often the very cheapest deals involve no flexibility whatsoever.

Too many people end up paying hundreds of pounds they cannot afford because they've fallen foul of the rules in the small print. They want to take luggage on holiday, or cannot print their boarding passes on their continental campsite, or need to eat on the journey. One airline – Samoa Air – has even introduced a scale of fares depending on what you weigh, on the grounds that their aircraft use more fuel if they have a lot of heavy passengers. One UK no frills service flirted with plans to charge passengers to use the toilet and having cheaper fares for those who didn't mind standing for the flight, but these ideas have been dropped for the time being.

Travelling light and with cases that meet airline dimensions for hand baggage (using the little frames to check once you get to the airport may be too late) can save a family of four as much as £200 on some routes and airlines.

There are bargain flights very early in the morning and very late at night, but you need to make sure you can get to the airport or get home at awkward times. A taxi fare will often wipe out any saving and you're likely to end up very tired if you miss a night's sleep, which isn't conducive to a jolly holiday or going back to work the next day. Fares are also usually cheaper mid-week so it may be worth considering a Tuesday to Thursday short break or a Tuesday to Tuesday holiday.

Use travel comparison websites – the main ones are listed in the Appendix.

The key things you're interested in, however you book, are:

- What does the fare include?
- Is it a return fare?
- How far is the airport from the town or city you want to visit? Don't assume because it has, say, Barcelona in the title that it's in Barcelona. How much will it cost to get to your final destination?
- What are the charges for hold luggage, checking in at the airport, not checking in online, choosing your seat in advance, extra leg room, or using a credit card?

CREDIT CARDS AND AIR FARES

Airlines usually make customers pay the credit card transaction fee or administration charge and you may also be stung with a booking fee.

It's still worth booking with a credit card because if the airline does not deliver the tickets or cancels your flight then you can make a claim for a refund through the credit card company if the cost was more than £100 and less than £30,000 (under the Consumer Credit Act).

AIRPORTS ARE EXPENSIVE PLACES

In an airport, food costs more than on the high street. Duty free is rarely a bargain compared to ordinary shop, supermarket or pharmacy prices. Take a picnic, but remember liquids cannot be taken through security except in very tiny amounts. Make sure that your picnic bag won't fall foul of luggage rules.

Travel money is most expensive at airports. Make your arrangements in advance using an online comparison site. Choose a payment card that has no foreign surcharge. Take more than one card with you just in case one of the banks has a technical meltdown when you're abroad. If you need more cash use your debit card to withdraw it. Travellers' cheques belong in the dark ages.

When you get on the plane it does not get any cheaper if you're flying 'no frills'. You will have to pay for drinks and food and a toasted sandwich is likely to be a lot more expensive than in corner cafes. Alcohol, soft drinks and tea and coffee will all need to be paid for too.

AUTOMOBILES
MOTORING COSTS

The most popular way of getting to work is by car, or van, with some 15m workers across the UK driving, compared with 4.3m using public transport, according to the Office for National Statistics.

We often have no idea what we're paying per mile or per year – in total – as we pay so many different motoring bills. Many people will be using their cars in the mistaken belief that it's cheaper than taking the train. This is partly because of our love affair with cars and also because we don't count all the costs of running them.

Driving costs will vary according to the model of car and the mileage you do. The Automobile Association calculated the average charges (the costs you have to pay to keep the vehicle on the road) for a car costing up to £13,000 to buy and these are shown in the table below.

VEHICLE STANDING CHARGES

MILEAGE	STANDING CHARGE	PETROL, TYRES, SERVICE, REPAIRS, PARKING AND TOLLS	TOTAL PER MILE	TOTAL PER YEAR
Up to 5000 miles a year	45.35p a mile	23.3p per mile	68.65p	£3432.50
Up to 10,000 miles a year	22.92p a mile	23.3p per mile	46.22p	£4622

Car running costs are never cheaper per mile than a season ticket and are unlikely to be cheaper for an off-peak longer journey. A one-off peak time journey may cost more per mile than the car but don't forget parking and any congestion charges.

We like to believe that having a car for social and leisure use will more than pay for itself compared to public transport and taxis, but that's only likely to be the case for people who live deep in the countryside.

The other thing we like to believe in is the miles per gallon (MPG) publicised by the manufacturer of our chosen vehicle, but this is another area where we are being regularly conned. For example, in April 2013 the Advertising Standards Authority upheld a complaint against one manufacturer from a car buyer who claimed that the advertised MPG for the make and model was unachievable. The car company in question admitted the figures could be misleading and did not reflect real driving results.

The way you drive can cut the cost if you reduce your speed and drive at a steady pace but this isn't always within your control. You can offer to car share with a colleague in return for a fixed contribution to the petrol. Don't leave it to occasional donations or it can be embarrassing – they will be saving money and you have to fund your car insurance, etc.

In most major towns and cities parking savings can be made by using park and ride schemes. The parking is often free and the bus fares are usually cheaper than parking in a town or city centre. It does not have to be a formal scheme – many people park on any streets that don't have parking restrictions and then walk or take a bus. This makes an even bigger saving for London drivers if they can manage to park outside the congestion charge zone and save themselves £10 a day.

Whether you need it for work or for pleasure and leisure, running a car is expensive. The younger you are and the newer the car then the more expensive ownership will be. Car insurance for under-25s can cost more than the car is worth. At the time of writing average car insurance for 17 to 20 year olds is £2900.

BUYING A NEW CAR

Brand new cars automatically lose value as soon as they leave the showroom. Depreciation – the difference between what you pay for a car and what you get when you sell it on – is the biggest cost after petrol for most motorists. A new car will typically have a residual value of 40% of its purchase price after three years. This is an average 20% loss a year, or £3200 on a £16,000 car.

Depreciation will vary depending on the car bought, the miles driven and whether newer models have been launched. Generally depreciation slows after two years and by five years most of the depreciation is done – this makes nearly new cars better value than new ones.

Some drivers want to have the newest, brightest, smartest cars and feel that the improved fuel efficiency, the offer of three years of free service and no MoT tests will be enough to balance the depreciation. Check out the terms of any warranty on a new car and the actual fuel efficiency as rated by independent motoring sites and magazines. As mentioned earlier, few cars achieve the astonishing rates advertised.

Check out the emissions, as a clean car may reduce the cost of road tax and even residential parking permits. Don't take on the showroom's finance without checking it out thoroughly and looking at the alternatives – even if it claims to cost 0%.

Ask for a discount on the vehicle price or, failing that, for extras to be thrown in. It's surprising how often there's a better deal available if you press the salesperson on this.

Before you even visit the showroom get a quote for your insurance. Don't leave it until you have bought the car as you could get a nasty shock. Do full research and get quotes from price comparison sites.

The showroom may offer you a first year deal on insurance and you need to know whether it's a competitive rate.

BUYING SECOND HAND

Sellers of second-hand cars will try to persuade you that they've looked after the car, that it has a low mileage and that it has been serviced properly. Remember, no one is what they appear when they are selling second-hand cars. They are not your friend and to them the sale will be more important than honesty.

You need to be fighting fit to get good value for your money. All car sellers have tricks up their sleeves to part you from as much money as they can. Private sellers and used car lots have as many potential downsides. Cars from dealers tend to be more expensive and faults may have been disguised, but you have more rights dealing with a professional.

Don't be fooled. Too often the "private seller" is a dealer who sells from home to avoid the rigours of consumer law and the notice of the local trading standards department.

Low mileage improves the value of a car but buyers have to be confident that the mileage on the odometer is genuine. The average mileage for a car is 10,000 miles a year and it's not unknown for sellers to tamper with the mileage on cars that have done a lot more to bring it down to the average figure.

It's illegal to lie about a car's mileage. To avoid being suckered check the MoT certificate or the service record to see what the mileage was when the car was last in a garage. If the seller is the second or third owner it might be possible to find out from the earlier owners what the mileage was when they sold the vehicle.

Also check the pedals, steering wheel and seatbelts for signs of wear. It is even more suspicious if the car has a new steering wheel or pedal rubbers.

If you're not an expert on cars get one on your side. The main motoring organisations offer a checking service starting at about £20 per car and becoming cheaper if you check a few vehicles. The check will cover whether the car has been written off, stolen or was bought with a loan that has not been paid off. As crazy as it may seem, if you buy a car that has not been fully paid for by the previous owner then you become responsible for the loan. The check fees include insurance so that if they don't spot a problem you can claim from the checker instead of the car owner. You can also pay a modest fee to find out if the vehicle is roadworthy and to find out if it has been subject to a safety recall by the manufacturer.

Use online price guides to give an idea of what you should pay. The older a car and the lower its price the more likely a professional check will find bad news that stops you buying. Remember, you're not only preventing yourself from being ripped off – you're making sure the vehicle is safe for you and your family.

Cars can be subject to identity theft. In other words, the number plates and even the log book (V5C registration certificate) may be for different cars. The person trying to dispose of the vehicle may not have covered their tracks completely, however, so look out for things that don't match – such as the colour of the car as detailed in the log book not being the same as the colour of the car in front of you.

Also check the vehicle identification number (VIN), or chassis number. It's possible that the vehicle you're considering buying is not stolen but has been in an accident and is actually two (or more) cars welded together, so check the VIN tallies in all locations as well as with the number on the log book.

The VIN is a combination of letters and numbers and can be found on a metal plate in the engine compartment and elsewhere on the car. Newer cars also have it on one of the windows. You can often find details about where to look on a specific vehicle if you search online for the make and model details and add the words "VIN location".

PETROL

Petrol prices keep on rising year on year, though there was a respite in the autumn of 2013. The pattern is one of continual price rises because there's little competition in many parts of the country and on motorways. The average cost of a litre of petrol increased by 59% between January 2007 and March 2013, from 87.3p to 138p. On motorways it can be around 10p a litre more and prices are sometimes positioned so that drivers can't make a decision until after they've left the motorway and pulled into the garage. It is proposed at the time of writing that the prices of petrol should be displayed before you leave the motorway, but there is no timetable for this change.

The price of petrol has gone up so much that official records show that we are driving fewer miles. As we write, allegations of price manipulation of the petrol market are being investigated after major oil companies were raided by the European Commission.

But don't hold your breath for prices to come down.

The best deals tend to be offered by supermarket garages and these sometimes offer 10p a litre off petrol when customers spend £50 or £60 in the store first. It isn't worth buying groceries from somewhere you would not normally visit for the vouchers and definitely not worth travelling miles to a garage to get the deal. For example, if you bought groceries at Haywards Heath in Sussex the nearest Sainsbury garage is in Hove, some 18.5 miles away. Google Maps says the average cost of the round journey would be £5.16 which is more than the saving you could make at 10p per litre on a tank of petrol for most cars. As ever, weigh up any deals carefully.

You can increase mileage per gallon by keeping your tyres properly inflated, not carrying unnecessary items in the car or boot, and even keeping the car clean (honestly).

CAR INSURANCE

Car insurance is a legal requirement. While, for reasons mentioned earlier, premiums fell for the first time in 19 years in 2013, it's still a significant expense.

Spend time on the money comparison sites to get the best deal. You can reduce the cost by limiting the number of drivers, the number of miles, increasing the excess you're willing to pay and putting the vehicle on a driveway or in a locked garage every night.

Insurance should no longer be cheaper for women than for men. The young and inexperienced driver can also get cheaper cover by having their driving monitored by a black box, so long as they drive carefully. You must never lie about who the main driver is or what they use the vehicle for. This will allow the insurer not to pay out in the event of a claim.

Never accept the first quote. This is particularly important for renewals. Companies keep their best rates to attract new customers, but if you challenge the renewal figure they may reduce it or you may have to move and to become a new customer for another company.

Once again you need to allow time to do the research and get the new insurance before the first company automatically renews your cover. If it does so it will take you days or weeks to get the money back and this may send you overdrawn.

- If you have a no claims discount it's worth protecting it.
- Keep the insurance details in your car so that you are prepared should the worst happen.

THE CAR INSURANCE CLAIM GAME

Making sure you have the right motor cover and driving carefully isn't enough to win the battle if you have to make a claim. You need patience, plenty of time and full details of the incident. If possible take photographs of all vehicles concerned with your (smartphones are handy for this). Give your insurance details to the other driver(s) and get theirs. If they are driving commercial vehicles photograph the company details.

If it's a serious accident and your car cannot be driven then you will need to contact your insurer from the roadside and the costs will begin to mount. The number they give out is a premium rate one that costs up to 40p a minute to call from a mobile and they will tell you the company they will use to transport your vehicle from the scene of the accident. The car will be taken to their preferred repairer for assessment.

Whether you are to blame for the accident or an innocent party, unless you have a nearly-new vehicle a surprisingly large number of damaged cars are estimated to be not worth repairing and written off. This happens because the insurer undervalues the vehicle before its accident and the repairer estimates the cost of repair using expensive replacement parts from the original manufacturer rather than perfectly safe, generic, cheaper parts. They also estimate that it will take a long time to carry out the repairs. In this way the mechanic can manage to tell the owner that a car, valued at say £3300, will cost £3330 to repair and is therefore written off. Once the excess is taken into account the insurer may offer £2800 in settlement... but, of course, you cannot replace a car you paid £5000 for with £2800.

Therefore, don't accept the first offer. While the insurer is unlikely to increase the payout to the level you need to replace the car, you should be able to get a little bit more. You don't have to even accept a revised offer though. You could also ask the repair shop where the car has been taken what it would cost to repair the vehicle safely as a private deal using generic parts. This could be a lot cheaper in our example. An alternative is to ask a reliable repair shop that you know of for a quote.

If you are doing this you need to find out from the insurer what type of write-off it is. If its category C or D then you may be able to arrange to have the car repaired, but you will have to buy back your vehicle from the insurer. In the above example, which happens to be a real one, the insurer offered to pay £2300 in full settlement. The car was then repaired for £1600, including the new MoT (which is required for some write-offs) and the vehicle identity check (which is also mandatory in some cases).

At the end of it the driver had a few hundred pounds in hand, but the value of the car was lower. If it was a category C write-off and the owner wants to sell it later the price will be affected because the log book is marked that it has been written off and repaired. The advantage is that you have a car that can be used and all being well your insurer will pay for a hire car while the repairs take place. You also have an MoT for a full year.

If the car is a category A or B write-off this route isn't allowed as it's deemed that the vehicle is too badly damaged to repair.

Even if the car isn't written off, you need to allow time during the working day or in the early evening to call your insurer to progress your claim. If you can, make the calls from a landline. If you don't have access to a landline, find out the non-premium phone numbers for contacting the person handling your claim. The calls can add up to hours of waiting time – for which you are charged – listening to dreadful music.

When you get through to the claim handler have all your information to hand – policy number, claim number, date of birth, date of accident, etc. If you're too busy at work to spend hours chasing up your claim you can ask another family member to do so, but you will need to tell the claim handler you're authorising someone to do this and you need to give their date of birth, maiden name, middle name, address and whatever other information the company requires.

Always get the name of the specific person handling your claim and correspond with them directly. Be friendly as this will pay off in terms of better service, but do let them know of your frustration with any delays. It's surprising how often they will endeavour to speed things along.

BREAKDOWN COVER

If you have an older car or do a lot of motoring a long way from home you should consider breakdown cover. This can be a cost-effective add-on to your car insurance and sometimes comes as one of those extras with your bank account – so check before you buy it separately. Some new cars come with a year's free breakdown cover (as you are unlikely to need it).

The AA and the RAC are traditional providers but there are a range of alternatives these days. Don't just look at price but check out user reviews about how efficient they are and how quickly they typically turn up at a breakdown.

There are a whole host of cover options, including cover if your car won't start while you're still at home, which can be useful for an older vehicle. Keep an eye out for introductory offers that can more than halve the price and may give you vouchers for high street stores as well.

OTHER WHEEL DEALS
BUSES AND COACHES

Travelling by bus can be cost effective but you need to do local research as many towns have hiked fares in recent years. Fares can also vary between service operators and there may be an alternative such as rail travel. You should also check where bus fare stages start and end. You may find the bus stop slightly further from your house works out cheaper because it takes you into the next fare stage and nearer your ultimate destination, or you could try getting off the bus early on your way home if this will mean you are alighting in a cheaper fare zone. As with trains, bus passes can dramatically cut the cost of regular travel.

Coach fares can be very competitive but, as with trains, factor in holidays when working out the cost of season tickets. Some people worry about coaches not keeping to time the way trains do but given the appalling delays some rail commuters suffer we're not sure how much of a downside this is.

When it comes to leisure travel by bus or coach, they can offer similar advance off-peak deals and have services travelling through the night, which some hardy souls regard as a bargain as they can sleep on board instead of paying for accommodation.

Megabus (operated by Stagecoach) can be a very cheap way of travelling, particularly midweek, with fares starting from £1 plus a 50p booking fee. Check it out on **www.megabus.com**.

Megabus also operates Megatrain services (**www.megatrain.co.uk**), which can be purchased from the same website. These fares also start from £1 with a 50p booking fee and are available on selected peak and off-peak East Midlands Trains, South West Trains and Virgin Trains services. For instance, you may be able to get from London to Sheffield by train for £1.50, if you are flexible about when you travel.

HIRING A CAR OR VAN

Whatever the initial hire quote, the price will be more. There will be additional insurance per day, mileage surcharges and the price they charge for the petrol. The location of the hire depot will also have an influence on the price you pay per day. It will usually pay to take a taxi to a hire branch rather than hire at an airport or station.

Don't agree to additional insurance without thinking about it. This can often cost more than you would pay if you have a minor accident and the chances are you won't have an accident. If you refuse extra insurance for the bodywork make sure you check and log with the hire company all the damage already on the vehicle.

If you book a car online and find that the model you booked isn't available you should not be charged for a larger vehicle, but sometimes the hire firm will try to charge more, and the running costs will be more. Refuse any surcharge. The lack of the cheaper vehicle is their fault.

There are two scams with petrol. One is at the outset of the hire deal and the other is at the end. Some hire firms insist that you take a full tank of petrol and pay for it at their designated price even though it's unlikely you will use all the petrol. They encourage you to return the vehicle empty, but know that people won't risk running out of petrol on the journey back so they will always win.

The second money maker for hire firms is to expect the driver to return the vehicle with a full tank of fuel and if it isn't they will charge for however many litres the car is underfilled by at a premium price.

There can also be penalties for not returning the vehicle clean inside and out. New charges are invented all the time. Read the small print and take time to read the contract, not just the bits that are circled for you to sign.

CAR CLUBS

In large cities there are car sharing clubs, which cost up to £200 a year to join and then charge you per hour when you use one of their cars. The price per hour will vary according to location, the model of car, and when you want to use it.

These schemes can save you a lot of money compared with owning a vehicle if you don't use your car much, but there's a risk that a vehicle won't be available when you want one. It works best for those who plan ahead. You save on depreciation, insurance, car tax, MoT and often have a newer car available to you than you could otherwise afford. You can even use the vehicle for a few days if you book ahead.

BICYCLES

More people are using bicycles to commute and to shop. The initial costs can be anything from a few pounds to thousands.

You should talk to your employer about the Cycle to Work Scheme. Introduced in 1999, it enables employers to provide bikes as a tax-exempt benefit. Employees effectively rent the cycle from their employer with an option to buy and it covers bikes and equipment up to a £1,000 limit. For more information go to **www.cycletoworkalliance.org.uk**. If you're thinking of using a bike for part of your train commute, check out when you can actually travel with a bike on the train as there may be restrictions.

Many household insurance policies don't cover bikes worth more than £250 so you will have to notify your insurer if your bicycle cost more. You also need a good lock, particularly if you're going to leave it in a central town or city location. These can cost up to £100 but are worth it.

In London you can hire bikes at stations and other central sites. Regular users can pay £90 a year and then pick up a bike whenever they need one. The first 30 minutes of cycling is free and many journeys fall into this category. There are penalties for damage or not returning bikes on time.

TRAVEL INSURANCE

If you're travelling to European member states it's worth applying for the European Health Insurance card (EHIC), formerly known as an E111. It's entirely free. But if you type 'E111' or 'European Health Card' into Google, you could be directed to a number of unofficial sites that charge you a hefty fee for your application. To get it free apply through the Post Office (**www.postoffice.co.uk**), at a high street Post Office, or call 0300 330 1350, which is a free number. The card gives free or reduced price health treatment across Europe.

Lots of things can go wrong on holiday so it's worth taking out travel insurance to cover your possessions, delays and forced cancellation. However, travel insurers will wriggle like slippery snakes to get out of paying. The Icelandic volcanic ash cloud was a case in point. A survey carried out by the *Daily Telegraph* and published in June 2013 exposed that 12 out of the 15 major travel insurance policies did not include volcanic ash-related claims on their basic policy without an extra fee.

Some bank accounts, credit cards, store cards and household insurance policies automatically include travel insurance. Check out the details. These policies often stop covering adults at age 64 and children when they reach 18 or 19, or leave home.

Travellers who have a pre-existing medical condition may also have problems getting cover. In 2013 a comparison website was set up to help the over-65s and those with conditions to find travel insurance. It is called **medicaltravelcompared.co.uk**. Saga, AllClear and **www.biba.org.uk** should also be able to help.

If you decide to pay for a one-off policy or an annual policy, check out exactly what will be covered. Lots of holidaymakers find out too late that their watch, iPhone or cameras were not covered because they exceeded the individual item limit, when really these are the items you want to be protecting when you take the policy out. Item limits can be set as low as £200. Policies might also have a limit for valuables collectively, which isn't much higher.

Insurers can also be very slippery when it comes to how they apply the insurance excess. At least one bank that offers 'free' travel insurance as part of an account package applies a £30 excess to *each part* of the claim. So if your bag was stolen and it contained your phone and your purse, that would be 3 x £30. The only way around this was to pay an annual excess waiver. So the 'free' insurance certainly isn't free in this case.

To be truly fighting fit for holidaying you should also find out what your household insurance covers. You may be able to reduce your travel cover if items such as cameras have *all-risks cover* outside the home on your contents policy. You should have a leaflet with all the details but if you can't locate it check online or ask for a new policy document to be sent to you.

As per our advice on insurance earlier – check what the excess is, are there item limits on payouts and think about what might happen to your premiums if you claim. Do you have separate cover for your smartphone and will it apply abroad? Your travel policy might not cover your phone and insurance providers have been censured for not keeping up with the times. As mentioned before, some people decide to only take a cheaper mobile with them on holiday and to leave their expensive technology secure at home, together with their expensive watch and jewellery, so that they can properly relax on the beach. For others a holiday would not be complete without their gadgets.

If you're taking out travel insurance don't opt for the policy offered by the company that sells you the holiday, unless you have done your research and found that it's good value. Usually the airline or travel company charges top dollar for their travel insurance and it offers poor value.

Before you apply for travel insurance take a minute to think about your medical history and that of your family. You may not know that you are suffering from an illness because your headaches or tingling hands were dismissed as nothing by your GP, but insurers sometimes expect you to know better than your doctor. There are lots of exclusions for previous conditions, age, travelling when pregnant, and many more. The insurers don't want to pay out.

When filling out the application form make sure you include every relevant fact. They will want to know of any reason you might have to cancel your holiday and make a claim. If in doubt, contact them and ask what they need to know – but avoid the premium phone lines when doing so.

Then, when you set off on holiday take the policy document with you so that you have the emergency phone number to call and the policy to prove you have cover if you do need medical treatment on holiday.

DON'T THINK TRAVEL – THINK MILITARY LOGISTICS

Every day we win a major battle. We get the kids to school. We navigate rush hour traffic or public transport that squashes us in like sardines (but charges us caviar prices for doing so). Every day is a little victory, but often it's more by luck than by judgment.

Most of us don't think sufficiently about whether the car we fill up with petrol is fuel-efficient or a gas guzzler. Often a journey to work and our means of transportation just happen to be the first option we worked out, the route we discovered during our first week in our new job, or what we think is the easiest solution. When was the last time you took different routes or types of transportation to work and compared them?

When we find a holiday we like our first question is liable to be "Can I afford it?" and not "Is this the best deal I can get?" Are you really wedded to that particular hotel in that particular location or have you just run out of steam looking?

Travel is a pretty critical part of our day-to-day lives and increasingly demands more of our budget to fund it – whatever mode of transportation we prefer. Much of our travel isn't optional and it deserves to be handled like a military campaign.

When Napoleon Bonaparte invaded Russia in 1812 he assumed it was going to be a campaign much like any other. However, his army was smashed by the atrocious winter weather. His logistics weren't up to the task. He failed to take into account how cold it was going to get and how stretched supply lines were going to become. Don't make the same mistakes.

First of all – conditions change. What may have been the smart option last year may not be the smart option this year. Have fares gone up, have service providers changed? Have bus routes altered, or have they taken some of the non-stop services off your train route?

❝ WHEN WAS THE LAST TIME YOU TOOK DIFFERENT ROUTES OR TYPES OF TRANSPORTATION TO WORK AND COMPARED THEM? ❞

Marshal your forces – this could be anything from car shares to negotiating a variation in your working hours. Ask other people how they get to work – they may know a back route if you're travelling by car, be up for a car share or know a better bus.

Imagine that you needed to get a whole army from A to B. Think how all those minutes and pennies saved would add up. Think like a military commander.

Take control of your travel rather than feeling like a victim of it. If your local travel company is planning to axe a valued route or particular train, do something. Complain to the company, write to the press, organise a petition...

Don't take travel lying down.

PROFIT!

ROUND 6

FINANCING THE FUTURE

SOCK!

"Look for intelligence and judgement and, most critically, a capacity to anticipate, to see around corners."

COLIN POWELL, AMERICAN STATESMAN AND GENERAL

Surviving the here and now is a battle, especially if we don't fight back against the evil forces trying to exploit us and rip us off. To truly win we need to plan ahead for every stage of our lives.

It can seem like a treadmill if you're always trying to catch up. The secret for planning for all our life stages is to start early. As you start work you should already be thinking about the rest of your life. Then you have a much better chance of enjoying each possible stage:

- Setting up home.
- Finding a partner and starting a family.
- Educating and launching children.
- Retirement (or winding down towards it).

You may have other stages in your life – launching your own business, or changing careers for example. There may be other unforeseen things along the way, such as divorce, redundancy or even long-term care. While no one wants to plan for these, if you have assets behind you then you can survive and maybe even prosper.

Most of us imagine how our lives may develop but very rarely do we try to anticipate the cost of upcoming stages. Take setting up a first home. Most of us know when it's time to leave the family nest or when sharing with other people loses its appeal. That first home of your own is likely to involve a rented property, so you'll need not only a deposit but enough money to buy furniture or bedding and items to brighten the landlord's furniture.

When you start to think of buying not renting, it's good to have some idea what prices look like. The average house price in the UK in mid-2013 was £238,000. In London the average was £375,000. The figures are daunting, particularly to those on the average wage of £26,000 or lower.

It's not just a question of what things cost but also what we like to spend on them. Weddings are said to cost an average of £20,000 nowadays and the costs can be much higher.

If you're thinking of starting a family we're not suggesting you should be put off by the practicalities – but we are suggesting you're prepared for them. The latest annual Cost of a Child report by insurance company LV= indicates that a child costs an average of £222,458 to raise to adulthood. Childcare is estimated to be £63,738 per child and that takes into account that children in England are entitled to 15 hours of state subsidised nursery education from the age of three. Uniforms, after-school clubs and university costs account for £72,832. Even pocket money adds up to £4,458 over the years.

Funding the cost of retirement has become more problematic in recent years because we are all living longer. We need to work out how much we need to save to fund the sort of retirement we want. To retire at 65 on a company or private pension of £12,000 a year to supplement your state pension you're likely to need a fund in excess of £200,000. If you want it to be inflation-proofed as well it will be at least another £100,000, or a much smaller starting pension.

Even if you can't get your head around full-blown retirement, consider how long you can keep up the same pace. If you have a stressful or physically demanding job you may need to think about winding down before retirement age and the impact that will have on your saving and spending power.

The whole lifetime package can be daunting but preparing for the future starts with just two basic steps.

1. If your employer offers a pension scheme join it. Don't delay.
2. Start to put some of the money you save by being a Money Fighter into a savings account where you cannot get it out too easily.

WHEN TO START SAVING

We know this is going to sound like stating the obvious, but the main secret of saving is to take the money out of easy reach, although that's harder in the online age. Work out what you could safely save without causing yourself problems. Is it the price of an extra latte each day or what you could save if you gave up cigarettes?

The latte savings could be £40 a month or £480 a year. The cigarettes could be £140 a month or £1,680 a year for a 20-a-day habit. Or maybe it's emptying your pockets and purse of small change each night. These can all add up quite quickly. If you incur expenses for work, such as by using your car or paying for parking, be diligent in claiming these back and think about saving the money. Next time you get a promotion think about saving half the pay rise for your future. Set up a standing order from your current account into a savings account on the day that your pay goes in. What you don't have, you don't miss.

If the money is put into a regular savings account – either in a tax-free individual savings account or an account that may offer twice as much interest for a fixed period – then there will be a penalty for making a withdrawal, but in extremis you can get at the money.

If you work for a company quoted on the stock exchange it will usually offer a share save scheme. These allow employees to buy shares at a discount after three years, five years or seven years. You can save from £5 up to £250 a month and at the outset of the scheme the price at which you can buy the shares is fixed. This is 20% less than the market price on the fixing day.

While there's no guarantee that share prices will go up the money is taken from your pay before you get it and you already have a 20% head start on the market, so as long as the price does not go down you will make a 20% gain over three years. Employees tend to do a lot better and there's no income tax to pay on the gain. You can make a profit of £10,900 on your investment in the year 2013-14 before any capital gains tax has to be paid.

Once you have the saving habit and are confident that you can squirrel money away without it causing you difficulty, begin to think longer term.

LONGER-TERM SAVING

Historically investing in property or shares has provided far greater gains than savings accounts. There are also tax advantages in that unless you're buying and selling shares as a business then the first £10,900 of profit is tax free each year and above that will be taxed at 18% or 28%. Your home is free of any tax as long as you don't own another property, and even then you can designate it as your main residence and avoid any tax when you sell.

The last decade has been topsy-turvy with volatile stock markets and falling house prices. The FTSE 100 (the index of the top 100 UK companies) was at 1417 at the outset in 1985. Ten years later it had more than doubled to 3689. At the end of 1999 – four years later – it was at 6930, a level that it has not been back to since. In 2002 it was back down at 3940 and ten years later it was 5898 and rising.

So you can see that choosing the right time to invest is difficult for an amateur. A crisis in the market is seen as a buying opportunity for the professionals but if you don't know what you are doing you can lose money fast. It can also take a very long time to make a return from investing in shares – it really is a long-term pursuit, meaning years or decades – so you should not invest money that you might need quickly in the stock market. As timing is so difficult it's best to drip-feed your money into the market at, say, £50 a month. Then you reduce the risk of putting all of your money in at a bad price.

With all investments you need to buy rather than be sold to and you need professional, impartial advice. Too often we fall victim to the salesperson at our bank or other financial institution. You need to be in control and do your own research. This can be done by looking at performance charts, or reading the material provided by the investment companies. You may even be lucky enough to have knowledgable friends. Remember, past performance is not a guide to future gains and if it seems to be too good to be true – such as banks selling investment products that guarantee you won't lose any money even if the market collapses – it could well be just that. Bernie Madoff made brilliant returns for his clients until his dishonesty was discovered.

Before you invest you also need to check the charges, fees, whether tax is deducted from the investment plan and if there are any penalties for withdrawing the money. There are proposals to simplify the charges but at the time of writing nothing has been agreed.

Those saving for their children often put their child benefit into a fund from birth to put towards their child's education and university costs. Over 18 years you're likely to do far better with such a fund than with a bank savings account, but if the market is down when the money is needed your gain will be reduced. The fund could also be used to help your child on to the housing ladder.

Many people regard their home as their pension pot and insurance against a rainy day. Their parents probably did very well with their investment in their homes but more recently this has not been the case… and you have to live somewhere.

A home buyer who bought a house in Greater London for £100,000 in 1983 would have a property worth £725,914 on average in 2013

– an increase of 625.9%. Those who bought a £100,000 property in 2000 would have seen an 87.6% gain and those who bought in 2007 would on average have seen a fall of 6% in mid-2013. The top properties in the top areas have escaped the downturn but outer London and less salubrious areas have had difficulties. Outside London, properties in northern England, Wales and Northern Ireland have seen double digit falls in prices with many executive apartments suffering the greatest drops.

Homes should not be regarded as investments. That said if you can get on the housing ladder you can save money as rents rise ever upwards and mortgage rates are at an historic low. If you manage to buy and have a spare room you can cover some of the mortgage by taking a lodger. Some only want a room Monday to Thursday night. You can charge as much as £4,250 a year for the furnished accommodation and pay no tax under the government's Rent a Room scheme. You will have to tell your lender and your insurer about your paying guest, though.

Many people put all their money into their home and that means they are 100% exposed to the vagaries of the property market. It's much better to put some money into investments or a pension scheme, some into a savings account and then, as for most of us, the lion's share goes into the home.

PENSIONS
PLANNING YOUR PENSION

Pensions are like gum shields – you only really value you them when you're about to be socked in the kisser. Why worry about pension planning when your retirement is so far off? But by the time retirement looms it's too late to plan and bam! We're floored by how little pension we'll get.

We're being expected to work longer and longer and it is increasingly being left to us as individuals to provide for our old age.

The sooner you reach for that gum shield the better.

As a rule of thumb and based on pension industry estimates, to ensure a reasonable pension on retirement you should have the equivalent of one year's current salary in your pension plan by the age of 35. This should rise over the next ten years to three times your current salary, and five times salary by 55. By retirement your pension pot should contain eight times your salary.

WORKPLACE OR COMPANY PENSIONS

If you are offered a workplace or company pension you will be a fool not to take it up, especially if it is one of the few remaining final salary schemes. These are virtually extinct in the private sector now but most public sector employees can still retire on an income that relates to their pay when they were in work, and the pension is likely to be index-linked (rising with inflation) into the bargain. Final salary schemes are sometimes called defined benefit schemes. What you get out is not related to what you put into the pension pot but to your salary while you were working and your employer has to make up any shortfall.

The type of workplace pension scheme you'll be offered these days is more likely to be a defined contribution scheme. Your employer (or employers, as you're bound to have more than one over the years) invests employee and employer pension contributions over the years until retirement and then the fund that's accumulated in your personal pot pays a pension based on its size. The pension paid also relates to the age of the retiree, their state of health and if they have a spouse who will need a pension when they die. What you get out is directly related to what you and your employer put into the pot and how the invested money performed over the years.

It's harder to avoid contributing to a company pension these days. The National Employment Savings Trust (NEST) was launched by the government in 2012 and will be rolled out to all employees, who are not currently offered a pension by their employer, by 2017.

Under the new scheme many employees will be auto-enrolled in their employer's pension. Not everyone will automatically enroll as this depends on age, how much you earn and whether you normally work in the UK. Introduction of NEST is being phased, targeting larger employers first. If you don't know what your employer pension options are you need to check now.

PERSONAL PENSIONS

Many self-employed people and some employees working for companies that don't offer pension schemes opt for personal pensions. Personal pensions have had mixed reviews over the years and have been mis-sold. Between the late 1980s and the mid-1990s a lot of people were wrongly encouraged out of good company schemes by financial advisors more interested in earning commissions from personal pension providers than offering sound advice to their clients.

But there are good personal pension options out there. The key is to get expert, impartial professional advice. As with anything else in this life, do your research and seek recommendations when finding a financial advisor and be prepared to ask lots of questions. The rules have changed (since December 2012) and your advisors must now clearly explain how you are paying for the advice you receive from them.

STATE PENSIONS

Your National Insurance contributions build up 'years' towards your state pension entitlement. You pay National Insurance when you work but you can also be credited with making contributions when you're raising a family and during periods of registered unemployment or sickness. You need to realise, though, that there is no pot of money with your name on it and no real indication what the state pension will be by the time you come to claim it.

The State Pension alone is not enough to fund your old age.

The main thing is to make sure you qualify for as much state pension as possible. You currently need 30 years' worth of contributions or credits to get the full basic State Pension but this will increase to 35 years for those who retire after April 2016. The amount you get will also increase.

The state retirement age for men and women is also on the move and will equalise in 2020 at 66. It will then move up to 67 from 2026. Many people won't get a state pension until a few years after they've retired from work.

KEEPING TRACK

It's important when you move jobs and homes that you give thought to your pension.

In the case of a company scheme it may pay to take your pension pot with you to your new scheme – you'll need advice. If you move to a new employer and leave your pension behind until your retirement day you may find that the company levies higher charges for the management of your pension pot than they do for continuing employees. It is worth finding out what the charges will be and whether it is worth transferring your pension fund to your new employer's scheme. If you need to transfer your money to another pension provider, check the fees charged and the recent performance of funds you are considering switching to.

You also need to keep checking who has your money. Mergers and takeovers of pension companies could leave your money stranded in a so-called 'zombie' fund with high charges and a lousy investment return. You can move your money if this is the case, so don't wait until retirement age to find this out. As we write there are proposals to limit the annual charges on pension funds but we are not holding our breath.

Company pensions, personal pensions and the state need to have your current address so they can contact you. Personal and company pension providers need details of your beneficiaries if you die. It may seem morbid to think about this but if you notify the scheme of your wishes then the money in the fund can be passed much more quickly to your relatives or other beneficiaries and not be taxed.

GETTING THE HIGHEST PENSION YOU CAN WHEN YOU RETIRE

Pension planning is a game of two halves. First there's saving for it (and making sure you save enough). Then there's making sure you get the maximum when you retire.

In the case of the state pension, anyone who does not have enough contributions can top them up. The Department for Work and Pensions (**www.dwp.gov.uk**) can be very helpful about how much you need to pay to improve your state pension. A good starting point is to see what you're entitled to so far by using the government's state pension calculator: **www.gov.uk/calculate-state-pension**

When you retire you'll have decisions about whether to take some of your personal or employer pension as a lump sum and how you use your pension pot to provide a retirement income. The financial company that's been looking after your pension pot isn't necessarily your best choice when it comes to providing your retirement income, so you'll need to get more professional advice and do more research at this stage. Here are some good starter questions:

- What pensions have I got and where are they?
- Should I start drawing on some or all of my pensions as soon as I can, should I wait a bit or stagger what pensions I draw and when?
- What lump sums can I get and what does that do to my retirement income?
- Do I want to use my pension pot to buy a pension for life (buy an annuity) or do I want to draw down from my pension pot, which may run out eventually? (You might

also choose to drawn down for a bit – particularly if you're looking at the best time to buy an annuity – see below.)

💥 Do I want to draw a lower pension to start with so that it increases as I get older and does the maths stack up (how long you might live versus how much you can start taking now)?

💥 What will be my tax situation in retirement?

A QUICK WORD ABOUT ANNUITIES

Most people use their pension pot to buy an annuity, which is an income for the rest of their life, guaranteed at the rate agreed when you buy it. You can also choose to have payments linked to inflation but the initial payments will be much lower. Sometimes the reduction for inflation-proofing is so great that it is reckoned the pensioner will have to live an awfully long time – more than 90 years – to be better off with inflation proofing than with getting a higher pension to start with.

Annuity rates have been falling in recent years. You have the right to check out annuity rates across the whole market and may find that you will get a higher pension from a company other than the one you saved with.

When you finally come to draw a pension don't delay once you have a firm quote. These are often only valid for 14 days and if you don't get the paperwork back in this time the rate can fall.

SURPRISES AROUND THE CORNER

Life has many surprises. We lose our jobs, have twins or triplets, illness or expensive weddings when we least expect them. If you start to make your money work for you and know where it all goes you will be better prepared than most.

REDUNDANCY

Losing your job can be a big shock even if you get a pay-off. First of all you need to make sure you get as much as possible in compensation from your employer. Check your employment contract to see what it says about losing your job. It may state that you should get pay in lieu of notice as well as redundancy money. If you are on three months' notice this payment makes a big difference. It has one downside – it will be taxed, whereas if the company is not contractually obliged to pay you for your notice period and chooses to do so this money can be counted in the £30,000 that can be paid on redundancy that is free of tax.

Your employer should pay for a solicitor as you prepare to sign your redundancy agreement. Even if they do not it is worth seeking legal advice either through a free service such as Citizens Advice or paying for a reasonably-priced solicitor recommended by a union, trade association, colleague or neighbour. They will be able to check that you are being made redundant legally and have not been discriminated against or unlawfully sacked. If your employer has not followed the correct procedure or has discriminated you may be able to get a bigger pay off or even keep your job.

Whatever happens, you should insist on a proper reference from your company. Your solicitor may even draft what you want it to say. Employers are often happy to go along with this as they are not trying to inflict unnecessary pain. It may be possible to negotiate that you work on for a little longer than some of your colleagues to help with the transition.

As soon as you know your job is ending you need to start looking for a new job. You may be angry but that is not the best way to set yourself on the road to getting another job. Your employer must give you support as you job hunt, including time off for interviews. While looking for a permanent job it is worth considering temporary work through a local agency. You will save money on commuting and it will allow you more flexibility to search for work and attend interviews. You will feel less pressured to take the first permanent job offered.

As it takes three months on average to find a new job you also need to have an emergency fund. If you do not have this money it is worth looking at raising some with a car-boot sale or garage sale. These can raise the spirits and clear the loft or garage of stuff you no longer use. Selling on eBay may also help you to raise money. Don't wait until things are desperate.

You need to plan, to find out whether you can get another job easily or whether this is the opportunity to start your own business, either as a freelancer working in your old industry, a sole trader or a bigger project. Find out what funding might be available and spend as little as you can as you start out.

KEEPING HOLD OF YOUR LUMP SUM

Once the redundancy payment is agreed you should sign on for Jobseeker's Allowance as soon as possible to conserve any lump sum. If you have no lump sum or it is very modest you may also be eligible for housing benefit or other means-tested allowances. Take whatever you can get. You have paid for it and do not know how long you will have to manage before a salary comes in again.

If you have been given a redundancy payment you also need to be on your guard against financial advisors trying to get you to invest straightaway, or the personal temptation to buy a new car, pay off your mortgage or go on holiday.

You need a new budget that pays for your essentials but which cuts back on your old in-work spending. You may want to feel as normal as possible but the nights out, clothes, golf, football or luxury foods can be forgone while you get back on to an even financial keel.

A survey in 2013 showed that cutting spending should be easier than you may think as a fifth of your wages are spent on going to work. Commuting costs, work clothes and office birthdays account for most, but lunches cost typically £58 a month, and tea and coffee £14.

PAYMENT PROTECTION INSURANCE

Banks and other lenders sell payment protection insurance to give you a regular income if you lose your job, but this product is expensive and rarely pays out. In fact, banks are now paying compensation to a large number of customers who were mis-sold this type of product.

If you want to create a cushion against hard times and unemployment, you are better off putting the equivalent of payment protection insurance premiums into a regular savings account while you're working. This will make sure you have a little bit of ready cash if the worst happens and you lose your job and get no compensation. Frightening statistics suggest that most of us are only a few weeks away from running out of money at any time; don't let this be you.

It is also important that we do not over-commit our salaries when we are in work. In the old days a big mortgage was eroded by house-price inflation and pay rises also helped to make repayments more affordable in just a year or so. Presently, pay rises have been constrained to below inflation rates and house prices are not currently enjoying meteoric increases in value. You have to think what would happen if you lost your job. If you are a two-salary household it may be less drastic than for a one-income family, but you need to have a plan.

> **STATISTICS SUGGEST THAT MOST OF US ARE ONLY A FEW WEEKS AWAY FROM RUNNING OUT OF MONEY AT ANY TIME.**

DIVORCE

The divorce statistics have been better in recent years, but many experts feel there is pent-up demand from couples who cannot afford to divorce because they cannot sell their homes. Divorce is a personal heartbreak and an even bigger financial one. As Money

Fighters we can feel at our most unguarded when the financial fight is taking place within the arena of an emotional breakup.

> **THE BIGGEST BENEFICIARIES OF DIVORCE TEND TO BE LAWYERS.**

In many cases one salary has to stretch to two households and even where both parties are working the cost of two homes is a burden, especially for those divorcing in their forties. While many men feel they are the biggest losers in divorce, divorced women are more likely to have a poor old age than married women, especially if they've taken time away from paid work, to raise children and not contributed sufficiently to a pension. While the years spent caring for children full-time do come with some state pension protection, going back into work part-time can penalise your state pension entitlement even more than being out of the workplace completely (due to not earning enough to pay NI contributions).

No one goes into marriage planning for divorce but it is important that couples who have assets before they are married make sure these remain theirs afterwards. More and more people are signing pre-nuptial agreements. It is also important that couples understand what each person brings to the relationship. Caring for children is as important as earning a salary. If you work together on a business then even if one person puts in the initial money the contribution of the other handling the books and manning the phones, say, needs to be taken into account. Remember, the biggest beneficiaries of divorce tend to be lawyers.

If you can work out what is a fair division of your assets and income going forward plus access arrangements for any children then the lawyers cannot play you against each other. Look at using mediation, where a third party tries to help a divorcing couple reach agreement amicably. This can save time and money. You do not have to be a wealthy oligarch to pay tens of thousands to a solicitor – all you need is a family home, a reasonable income and a heated dispute about who gets what.

Most divorcees feel they pay too much for the legal advice they get, yet probably are too upset to ask all the questions they should before agreeing to representation. You need to agree the costs upfront. The time to do this is when you are first consulting a solicitor. The better deal you get then the more you have to share between yourselves.

ILL-HEALTH

Some health problems can be avoided by regular exercise, eating healthily, drinking moderately and keeping your weight under control, but if it was always that easy very few people would ever get ill. You can be born with an unlucky gene, suffer from an industrial illness or be afflicted by all manner of illnesses without any warning.

Some employers will pay wages for up to six months when you are ill and that can be a tremendous help as state sickness pay is not generous. Banks and other financial institutions sell insurance that will pay out if you are ill, but there are often many exceptions. These policies are often sold on fear, can be expensive and may not pay out. Some only pay out if your illness is deemed to be critical, but often a life-changing (but not critical) illness does not count. Also, as ever, insurers try to get out of paying out. For example, if you suffer from frequent, severe headaches when you take out a policy the insurer may refuse to pay out if you find out a year later that you have a brain tumour.

If you are tempted to buy a policy make sure you tell the company everything and read the policy details. If your family has suffered from a particular illness it is worth checking whether it will be covered if you later suffer from the same illness. There have been positive changes recently, including the number of critical illnesses that will be covered, but just because there are a great number of conditions covered it doesn't automatically mean it is the best policy. The bulk of claims cover only a handful of conditions.

Workplace pension schemes can also offer insurance for employees who fall ill and cannot work again. These schemes cost the employees nothing and usually offer up to two-thirds of their salary until retirement age. In other cases you may be able to take an ill-health retirement and claim your work pension early.

When you are ill it is difficult to think about your finances, but it is essential that you or a relative keeps on top of your bills and income. You may be entitled to a means-tested benefit to pay your mortgage or to pay for special foods or extra heating that your condition requires. These are not easy to apply for or to get, but you cannot ignore your finances. For instance, too many cancer sufferers find that as soon as they are in remission they have to fight eviction or even bankruptcy. In this case you may be able to get help through Citizens Advice or Macmillan Cancer Support (**www.macmillan.org.uk**).

The ill-health that worries most of us even more than cancer is dementia. There are massive cost implications and you need to know that those who have your best interests at heart are in a position to help. You need to have a lasting power of attorney (POA), in which you nominate someone to run your financial affairs when you are no longer able to. Details are available on **www.gov.uk**. It costs £130 to register each lasting power of attorney with the Office of the Public Guardian. Solicitors can also make the arrangements. When one spouse is too ill to look after their affairs there can be serious problems as the other spouse will not be able to sell a jointly-owned home, for example.

If you do not arrange POA and succumb to illness then your affairs will be handled by the Court of Protection. This is costly and the service is poor.

DEATH

Okay, maybe it's a long way off and you have many more fighting years in front of you, but you need to plan for it. If you do not plan for your ultimate demise then your assets may not go where you want them to. This is particularly the case after divorce or if your assets are more than £250,000 in England, Wales and Northern Ireland and £473,000 in Scotland.

The first £250,000 goes to a spouse in England, Wales and Northern Ireland and then the other assets are split in two and the spouse gets half and the children or their children share the rest. In Scotland properties worth up to £473,000 go to the spouse.

One of the problems facing a lot of couples in recent years is that those who have not married or entered into a civil partnership are not entitled to any of their partner's assets when no will has been made. If you have no spouse or heir your property will go to either the Treasury or the duchies of Cornwall and Lancaster. In 2012 unclaimed assets of £38.5m went to these institutions.

MEET YOUR FUTURE SELF

Imagine you've teleported many years into the future. It's a bright sunny day, you're walking down a street and you meet your future self coming in the opposite direction.

How's life going for the future you? Okay? Better than okay? Brilliant?

Do they look happy? Do they look like they have the material things they need in life? They may be about to climb into a shiny red sports car or a clapped out banger. Do they have a hint of a suntan that indicates their last foreign holiday wasn't that long ago? Most people have trouble with this scenario. After all, who knows what the future may bring? You haven't got a crystal ball, right?

Well, you've actually got something far, far better than a shiny orb of glass. You've got your bank statements and your salary slips. There's the box on the shelf which has all the paperwork for your mortgage, your savings and a copy of your will (the original is lodged with your solicitor and everyone who should knows that's where it is).

To look into the future all you have to do is look at your financial present and make a few calculations. When will the mortgage be paid off? Do you have enough coming in to pay it off a little more quickly? How are your savings and investments looking? If your spouse/partner died (or left) could you cover all the bills? Based on your saving and spending now, what sort of nick are you liable to be in some years down the line? Do you want to be your future self based on the cold, hard, present-day facts?

The trouble is we get so caught up in what our present self wants that our future self is often very hard done by. Why worry about a pension some time far in the future when there's a golf club or a lovely pair of shoes deserving of our attention right now?

Like all of life, meeting the needs of our future self requires a little honesty, a little balance and a little imagination. What would it feel like if the future self walking towards you on our time travel expedition looked miserable, care worn, plain hard up? By all means enjoy today but plan for tomorrow.

Keep in mind that the ability of the state to provide is increasingly under pressure as the population ages and that the cost of essentials such as food, accommodation and utilities rise. Take a long-term, strategic approach. Provide for your future self and don't put all your eggs in one basket. Spread investments, consider balancing something slightly more risky (with the promise of a great return), with a block of low-risk options that won't make you rich and may well be eroded by inflation, but will give you a solid base.

When you make a financial decision, such as choosing to release some of the equity tied up in your home to fund a nice holiday, ask yourself the question: what will my future self think of this decision? Make sure their voice is part of any discussion. They'll thank you… eventually.

> **BY ALL MEANS ENJOY TODAY BUT PLAN FOR TOMORROW.**

ROUND 7

TAX

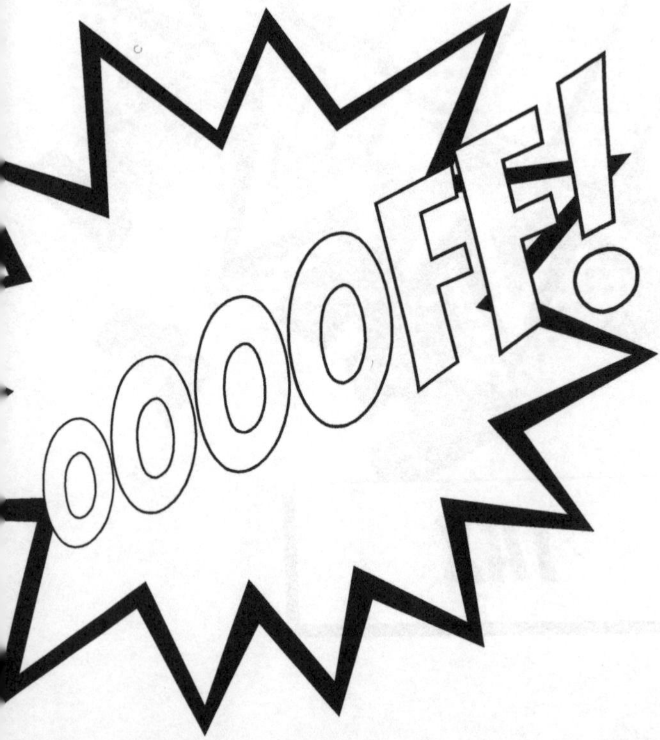
OOOOFF!

"We don't pay taxes. Only the little people pay taxes."

WEALTHY AMERICAN HOTELIER LEONA HELMSLEY, JAILED FOR 19 MONTHS FOR FEDERAL TAX EVASION

We hear daily of super-rich individuals and mega companies who pay very little or no tax while the millions of us "little" people – employees, the self-employed and pensioners – seem to pay an awful lot of it.

In 2013 Her Majesty's Revenue and Customs (HMRC) announced that more than 5m people had paid the wrong amount of tax in the 2012/13 tax year. Two million had to pay an average of £400 to £500 extra tax while 3.5m were told they had paid too much and were due a refund. Our view is that if HMRC were able to verify that this many people paid the wrong tax then the real figure is probably higher. So stay on top of your tax affairs and don't assume the officials will get it right.

The letters telling taxpayers that their accounts have been mischarged go out between May and October each year and finding out you've underpaid can deal a body blow to your household finances. It doesn't matter that employers and taxpayers have provided all the information HMRC require, it is your responsibility to notice if you are paying too little tax. It's your fault, not that of the tax professionals. To cap it all, if you get a bill for underpaid tax HMRC will charge you interest on the debt at 3% but if they've taken too much tax from you they will only pay interest on what they owe at 0.5%.

Those who haven't paid enough tax will usually have the additional tax deducted from their earnings in the following tax year – if the amount does not exceed £3,000.

The problems can lie with the tax codes issued in the spring each year. Anyone who gets a state pension will get a code early in the year and then get at least one more once the increase in their pension is verified. It isn't unusual for taxpayers to get three different tax codes in the same post. Anyone receiving a state pension is at risk of falling foul of the tax rules, so are people working more than one job to keep afloat. The state pension is taxable and if you have any other earnings or pensions then there's the opportunity for the Revenue to get its sums wrong.

Employees have little room for manoeuvre and are the easy targets for HMRC because they provide all the information required and are not trying to cheat the system. Even so, HMRC should not always win. If you're sent a letter demanding extra tax but you believe you have provided every bit of information that the Revenue needs and their assessment is wrong, call them out on it. They're not all-knowing and they don't always get things right.

In some cases an additional large tax bill can be written off if you can demonstrate you have done everything you can to pay the right amount and would face real hardship in paying any back tax. Unfortunately there have been so many people facing unexpected bills the Revenue has got tougher about which cases they will let go. To win you need good records. Keep every bit of paperwork relating to your tax affairs. It will protect you.

❝ KEEP EVERY BIT OF PAPERWORK RELATING TO YOUR TAX AFFAIRS. ❞

Remember, you're supposed to know how much you can earn before you pay tax in any year so make sure you do. It can get confusing because the Chancellor will give early notice of any goodies, such as improved tax allowances, announcing them up to 16 months before they are implemented.

MEET A FIGHTER...

John Kent made the headlines in the autumn of 2013 after a four year fight with HMRC over a £10,000 demand for unpaid tax. The former software engineer had retired in 2006 and alerted the taxman about his change in circumstances. Then in 2009 he received a demand for tax on his pension payments.

John took issue with this, given he'd kept the taxman fully informed. Initially HMRC reduced the demand from £10,000 to £3,300 but John kept on fighting and finally had the bill written off altogether. The *Daily Mail* quoted him as saying: "The way to beat them is through tenacity and persistence – never give up."

THE 2013-14 TAX PICTURE
INCOME TAX AND NATIONAL INSURANCE

In the year 2013-14 everyone could earn £9,440 (a personal allowance) before paying any tax. Those over 65 before April 2013 can earn £10,500 before paying tax, but if they earn more than £26,100 the slightly higher tax allowance is reduced back to £9,440. Those over 75 have a higher allowance of £10,660. Blind people can earn an extra £2,160 before paying tax.

The basic rate of tax is 20% and that's paid on the first £32,010 of taxable income. This includes interest earned on bank or building society savings. You pay tax and National Insurance when you earn the money, and if you save it you're taxed a second time. A higher rate tax of 40% is paid by those who have more than £32,010 of taxable income. Above £150,000 of income the rate goes up to 45%.

Of course, the standard rate of tax isn't really 20% because National Insurance contributions are also taken from your earnings. In 2013 for earnings above £109 a week NI is charged at the rate of 12%, up to £797 a week. Above that the charge is 2%. This gives a real tax rate for most of us of 32%.

Many believe the NI payments are contributing to the health service or their pension but they are wrong. It's just an extra tax going to the exchequer. None of your NI payments are being accrued to pay your pension. They are going to pay the pensions of the previous generation who are claiming those pensions now, which is a little bit worrying for all of us.

There's a concession that few people know about. If your earnings are just above the personal tax allowance and some of that income is from bank or building society interest you may qualify for a lower rate of tax. An amount of £2,790 of bank interest above the personal allowance can be taxed at 10%. You have to apply for this concession. Any interest is free of tax if your income is lower than the personal allowance.

Banks and building societies deduct tax from all our savings accounts unless we complete an R85 form stating that we are not taxpayers and give it to any bank or building society that holds our savings. If you don't fill out the form and tax is deducted it can take you months to get the tax back and because it's your fault you don't get any interest on the overpaid tax.

Make no mistake the law reckons you should be on top of it even though the Revenue isn't. The time you have to claim back overpayment was reduced to four years in 2012. This means if you have overpaid tax in the year to 5 April 2010 you have to make a claim before 5 April 2014. On the plus side if you have underpaid the Revenue can only claim back for four years unless they had already started their enquiries before April 2010.

To avoid problems you should check the P60 form your employer gives you in May or the statements from pension companies to make sure that everything you earn is being taken into account. If a mistake was made by your employer they may agree to pay the unpaid tax or at least help you to sort it out.

Contacting HMRC to rectify a problem or make an enquiry can be difficult. In 2012 the National Audit Office reported that 30m phone calls were not answered – 5,000 a day. Those that are answered can pay up to 40p a minute if they are calling from a mobile. These premium rates are being phased out but there is no promise to have more people on the phones so that we do not have to wait so long for human contact.

Those with complicated tax issues who try to sort them out through the post are likely to wait at least 15 days for a response, if they get one at all. Your letters should be sent to the tax office that deals with your employer and should include details of what you believe has gone wrong and your NI number. It isn't enough to wait for a response – if you don't hear anything you have to chase up.

In addition to income tax we also have to make sure we don't fall foul of the capital gains tax or inheritance tax rules.

CAPITAL GAINS TAX

Capital gains tax is regarded by some as a voluntary tax in that it's paid on gains over £10,900 in a year and any losses in the same tax year or previously can offset the gain. There are also lots of exemptions. The main one is your home, although if you own more than one property you have to designate which is your main residence. As we have seen with the example set by MPs, many people flip their homes so that a property suddenly becomes their main residence when they want to sell it.

Items that are regarded as 'wasting assets' also escape CGT. Fine wines, clocks and other valuables can be bought and sold without incurring tax. Once again it tends to be the super-rich that benefit from these tax rules.

Those who do incur CGT pay according to their income tax rate. Those who pay standard rate tax will pay 18% on a taxable gain so long as the profit does not take them into the higher rate of tax. Higher rate taxpayers are charged 28% on their taxable gains.

For the rich it pays to make taxable gains rather than have the money taxed as income.

INHERITANCE TAX

Where inheritance tax is concerned there can be problems if a property is valued at death at a certain figure but the executors fail to sell it at that level. The Revenue regards the earlier valuation as correct and does not offer an inheritance tax refund.

Inheritance tax is currently paid on inheritances above £325,000, but there are exemptions. Property handed to spouses is exempt. A married or civil partnership couple each has the allowance, which allows them to give their assets to each other and then when the second partner dies up to £650,000 is exempt of tax.

You can also beat the taxman if you give away assets seven years or more before you die, but there needs to be a formal record and you cannot give your home to a family member and continue to live in it rent-free. Any transfer of property needs to be handled with professional help if you're to avoid an unexpected tax bill.

The super-rich can also invest to avoid inheritance tax. Investing in forestry in the UK can avoid inheritance tax after two years as it will qualify for the business relief exemption. Typically investment starts at £100,000 and will also give tax-free income when trees are felled and timber is sold. The returns have been increasing, but cannot be guaranteed. Escaping inheritance tax is the big attraction.

You can also give away £3,000 each year exempt of tax and any number of individual gifts of £250. When family members get married parents can each give £5,000 as a gift and grandparents can each give £2,500 without these counting towards your estate after you die.

It's worth using every allowance going if your assets are worth more than £325,000 as estates worth more than that, or £650,000 after the second death, are taxed at the rate of 40%. This happens even if the main asset is the family home and can often mean that the children of the family cannot afford to live there unless they can take out a mortgage to cover the tax bill.

DODGE THE PUNCHES AND LAND A FEW OF YOUR OWN

The big tax stories of the last year or so have been about the massive corporations and wealthy individuals who not only avoided paying tax but have done so with a breath-taking arrogance and protestations of entitlement. They're doing nothing wrong they tell us. Personally, we don't have the words to describe how we feel about this. Well, not words you can publish in a book. Where does that leave the rest of us, the little people?

At this stage we want to draw on yet another boxing analogy. Don't think of yourself as little people. Think of yourself as a flyweight boxer. The fact is the flyweight doesn't take the punches – he dodges them. They are also prepared to punch above their weight on occasion. They're lean, mean fighting machines. They're feisty. We like this.

So as little people we have to make sure we're taking advantage of every legal opening to minimise our tax bills and be prepared to slug it out with the heavyweights in the tax office if we think they've got it wrong. You don't have to park your moral compass to reduce your tax bill. We'll leave that flagrant exploitation of loopholes to the fat cats.

As a flyweight we're always circling, looking for the opportunity to land a really big punch on the opposition. If you're sick of big business paying too little tax – shout about it! Badger your MP. Buy

> **YOU HAVE THE RIGHT TO BE RIGHT.**

from companies that aren't as arrogant or as shameless about tax avoidance. Make your views known.

One of the reasons we sometimes feel so worn down by our financial battles is because we believe that what we do has little impact. It's only saving a couple of pounds a week, etc. Why fight that big company over shoddy goods or poor service – they're bound to win. HMRC is massive and powerful, why should they listen to little old me?

Well, big organisations make mistakes and can be intimidated by widespread anger. In June 2013 Starbucks offered to pay £5m in 'corporation tax' to HMRC, its first such payment in four years. Okay, it's a drop in the ocean but it's also a step in the right direction and a direct result of public outrage.

The size of your tax bill may be keeping you awake at night but government ministers toss and turn because of their dwindling ratings in the opinion polls, not to mention the views of voters back in their constituencies. If you're going to pay your tax like a decent human being – act like a taxpayer!

Make the big guys quiver under the rain of your well-placed punches. There's no debate that you can't be part of. Thanks to the internet, making your views heard has never been easier. If you think the taxman has got it wrong, for goodness' sake check. You have the right to be right.

Avoid the punches by being fast on your feet – but don't be afraid to land a few punches of your own.

ROUND 8

NEVER BE BLINDSIDED

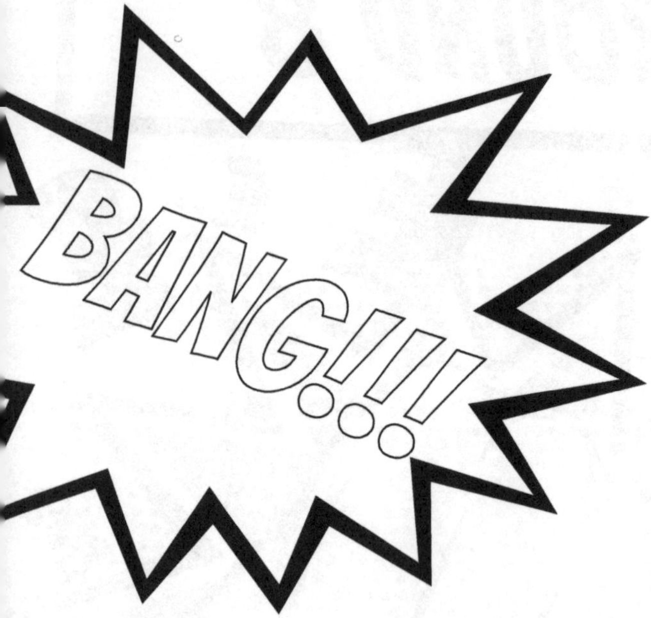
BANG!!!

"Sometimes, she had discovered, you had to walk around the holes in your life, instead of falling into them."

NATALIE O'REILLY IN BLINDSIDED, WRITTEN BY PRISCILLA CUMMINGS

This is a relatively short chapter but a really important one. To be truly fighting fit and defeat your financial opponents – including organisations, personal debts and wider economic factors, such as high interest rates – you have to be in control of any weaknesses you might have. Remember that everyone plays on these weaknesses to get you to part with money you do not have or do not want to spend.

The supermarkets deliberately create confusion to get us to buy more expensive packs when there are cheaper ones next to them. The banks bamboozle us with interest rates that cost us more than we expect when we borrow and pay us less than we want when we save. Fees can rapidly compound a small mistake with overdraft charges or penalties for withdrawing money at the wrong time.

Even the great financial disasters in history start with people failing (or choosing not) to see the danger signs, or forgetting the Money Fighter's mantra that something that seems too good to be true probably is. The 18th century South Sea Bubble disaster happened not just because a poorly-run company overextended itself and failed to take account of changing market conditions, but because investors parked their common sense in order to cash in on their greed. Well, it's a reasonable interpretation of what happened.

So not being blindsided is also about assuming that the worst can happen and asking yourself: how will I cope if it does? Whatever the bubble – house prices, stock markets, investments – sooner or later life will come along with a pin. Be ready. Be on your guard.

KNOW WHAT YOU HAVE TO SPEND

Knowing how much you have available to spend is more complicated than it sounds, otherwise we would all get it right all the time. Many of us think in terms of the salary we are offered when we get a job. We then get a shock when we get paid because once tax and National Insurance is taken out it is so much less, and then there are pension payments and maybe season ticket loans or back tax deducted.

> **WHATEVER THE BUBBLE, SOONER OR LATER LIFE WILL COME ALONG WITH A PIN.**

Even when we see the money in our bank account it is not really ours. There is a big chunk for your landlord or mortgage lender each month. Council tax is another fixed cost while gas and electricity vary with the season and can be devastatingly high at the end of winter. Water bills are growing. Travel to work takes another chunk. Telephone costs can bite us, particularly after a holiday or in a long-distance relationship. Insurance needs to be paid for. It's depressing when you deduct all these regular costs from your net earnings.

All these bills are before the flexible spending on groceries or other necessities is taken into account.

We have given you the tools to reduce all of the above and we hope the next few thoughts will help you to avoid the pitfall of being hit by overdraft charges that put you in the red for a second month and a second lot of charges because you did not notice that you have spent a few pounds too much. We also want you to avoid the high interest charges and penalty payments on credit cards.

KNOW WHERE THE MONEY GOES

If you know that there is never enough money to last the month then start the month as you intend to go on. Too many of us are dazzled by having a few hundred pounds in our bank account and shop like it will never run out. Look around at the checkouts in supermarkets at the very end of the month. There are more big shops because we all feel rich. There are more people in pubs, clubs, bars and restaurants and the clothes shops are busier. Lots of us indulge ourselves because we have worked hard and we are worth it.

Friends and family may not help. Many love vicarious shopping by being with someone who spends. They get some of the pleasure of acquisition with none of the hardship of having to balance their budget later.

SETTING A BUDGET

The best way to make sure that you do not overspend is to set yourself a budget for discretionary spends. Yes we need food but we can decide how much of the remaining money we can afford to spend, and more importantly check our cupboards, freezer and fridge and write a list before we set off so we do not buy things we already have.

We should not be too rigid or, like a diet, it will not work. Like a diet you should not shop when you are hungry or you will spend more. We all need treats and your list should allow for them, whether it be chocolate biscuits or your favourite cheese.

Lists also help us to avoid waste as we can plan for specific meals and plan how leftovers will be used rather than throwing them away before we go for the next lot of groceries. We waste 15m tonnes of food a year and 50% of that comes from our homes. More than half of this waste can be avoided. Never get blindsided by putting the freshest milk, yogurt, meat, cheese, at the front of the fridge so that the older food gets forgotten while you use the freshest. It may take a minute or two longer to put away groceries but you will not get any nasty surprises.

If you buy a chicken for Sunday lunch think about how you will use the leftover meat. Will it be risotto on Tuesday, sandwiches on

Monday lunchtime or salad on Monday evening? Or will you pop it in a clean freezer box, label it clearly and use it in the next week or so for a pie filling, curry or other family favourite? Remember, if you do not waste money on a bag of salad, a pack of yogurt and some cooked ham that you don't need you can probably afford to upgrade to a better cut of beef or some smoked salmon. Your grocery bills should also be cheaper.

So you decide what you want to spend on groceries and over the course of the month stick to it – without running out of necessities such as toilet paper or bread. You also need to decide what you will spend on clothes, going out, toiletries and make an allowance for presents. Christmas may only come once a year but far too many people are still paying for it the following December.

What is reasonable for you to spend on all of the above? If you earn £15,000 and have £500 a month in rent to pay then you cannot really afford designer handbags, however unreasonable this may seem. You really cannot afford to spend the best part of £100 on a night out when you take taxis, new clothes, drinks and food into account. However, you need to reward yourself or life is too miserable.

You should make the decisions up front about what you can afford – what is important to you will have a big bearing on this. If that very expensive handbag will be a one-off purchase that is half price in the sales and will be cherished for the next three years and it will not incur any interest charges on your credit card or overdraft fees then maybe you can arrange your budget to accommodate it. You will have spent your clothes budget for the foreseeable future on one bag so there can be no more purchases until the budget says you have some spending money.

If going out is important then you may have to pack lunches for work and avoid the coffee shops in order to have enough money to do this.

You're in control – or you should be.

SMOOTHING THE SPENDING LUMPS

A budget is what grandma had before credit cards were invented. She put away money every week in different jars or money boxes with several slots so that there was enough to pay for the gas bill, the winter coal delivery, summer clothes, Christmas and birthdays.

Now if we spend to the very last pound every month there is nothing there for the next month. Birthdays do not happen neatly every month. Your children do not grow out of, or wear out, their shoes at convenient times.

If you allocate money to specific spending needs or wants then you have a better chance of there being enough when you need it. You do not have to spend your budget each month. If you do not buy any clothes now there may be enough for a new coat later in the year.

KNOW THE PRICE OF (VIRTUALLY) EVERYTHING

Politicians are often ridiculed for not knowing the price of a pint of milk or a loaf of bread. When we all bought Mother's Pride sliced white loaves and had our full-fat milk delivered in glass bottles the question was fair. Now the 'value' sliced loaf is likely to be a third or a quarter of the price of the artisan granary loaf and there's a whole host of other breads and prices to choose from.

The same goes for different types of milk. Few of us have it delivered any more. Supermarket milk can be 90p for a single pint, £1 or less for two pints and it will keep to the end of the week. Buying three containers may be cheaper still, or a big six-pint container should be cheapest (but check).

While you should know what you are spending on your groceries, more importantly you need to keep tally of where the money goes.

First of all, there should be no surprises when we get to the checkout. We should have a rough idea of what we have spent and if the bill is a lot higher then there is no shame in asking for one or two items to be deducted.

Keep a running total. Work out what it is likely to cost before you go into the shop and only substitute items to save money, not because you have been tricked into thinking you will save money. It takes time but it puts you in control.

Many of us sweat over the big stuff and then lose control over the small items of expenditure. We cut our gas and electricity consumption, move to a cheaper supplier, buy vegetables when there is a seasonal glut and never pay full price for our clothes, and then somehow without being mugged we lose hundreds of pounds a month without a clear idea where it has gone. Some may be down the back of the sofa, but don't count on much of it being there.

All of us have areas of spending weakness. Is it the newspaper every morning? Or maybe you get tripped up by the soy latte on the way to the station. The lunchtime sandwich, the magazines, books, cosmetics, shower gels, etc., can get us all.

The first problem is that we either hand over a couple of coins or nowadays use a contactless card and it is so easy we do not count how much we are spending. Cards have made it very easy to spend a lot without realising it.

Do you know what the newspaper you buy costs? Do you buy chocolate or anything else when you buy your paper? How much do you spend on coffee each week? When you last went into Boots for toothpaste what did you spend?

We go to buy our morning paper and the sales assistant offers chocolate at half price or we are tempted to pick up a magazine. We reckon that we buy five soy lattes a week but we do not count in the fact that we sometimes get one on the way home after a hard day, or that we buy one for a colleague. A £13 coffee habit each week can easily become a £20 one. Knowing what you intend to spend and the price of each item is helpful so that you keep within budget. If you choose to spend £80 a month on coffee it cannot be spent on a new top or a night out.

You make the decisions.

YOUR MONTHLY MAINTENANCE

Factor the costs of monthly maintenance into your budget. Looking presentable for work – and socially – is no different to servicing the car, or keeping the gutters free of leaves so you don't end up with damp walls in your home. But we need to get value.

Hairdressing appointments are expensive for men and women but they are part of the deal if we want to look professional. Make sure you have appointments that give you the maximum benefit either socially or at work. If you are a party person then a Friday appointment is good. If work is your zone then maybe a Monday appointment is best as your hair will look good for most of the week. Buy quality clothes designed to last and take advantage of sales. Money Fight Club is not about doing without. It's about spending money wisely and getting what you paid for.

If you have a gym membership make sure you get value from this. You may be aware it is costing you £840 a year but what does that cost per visit to the gym? Would you be better off paying as you go? If you are not getting value would an off-peak membership work for you? These are usually considerably cheaper because gyms are often empty during the working day. The same goes for golf club fees or other sports costs.

You have to know where the money goes and more importantly feel you are getting value for it.

USING CASH

Debit cards, credit cards, store cards and charge cards make it too easy to lose track of what we are spending. You sign, put in your PIN or pass your contactless card across the terminal and it is paid for. So much easier than finding your purse, counting out the coins or notes and waiting for change. These cards seem to have an endless supply of cash, whereas our wallets and purses have a finite amount of cash. Using cash reconnects you to real money and makes

> **MONEY FIGHT CLUB IS ABOUT SPENDING MONEY WISELY AND GETTING WHAT YOU PAID FOR.**

you pay attention to what you spend.

If you are spending more than you want to, the simple way of reducing this is to work out what cash you can afford on incidentals and withdraw that amount from a machine once a week. You then know that is all you have to spend on odd purchases for the next seven days.

The lunchtime sandwich may have a drink and some fruit with it early in the week and newspapers may have another purchase attached, but if there is no money left by Thursday then you have instant coffee in the office, pack yourself sandwiches and read the newspapers online.

When things are tough try having cashless days – walk to work, avoid the shops. The point here is that you don't spend your cash and you don't spend other people's. It's not a cashless day if you let someone else treat you to your large latte plus friends will take a dim view if your lack of cash begins to regularly cost them money.

You will be amazed how well budgeting like this works and there are no nasty surprises when the bank statement or credit card bill arrives.

You decide how much you want to be in control. Making bank and credit card charges a thing of the past and having enough to buy the things you really want is reward enough for the tough cop you have to play with yourself.

If there are things that are better purchased with a card, keep a record of what you spend, particularly when things are going to be particularly tough – for example, if they suddenly cut back on your overtime at work. Out of sight out of mind is bad, bad, bad where our financial fitness is concerned. If you have a lot of cards in your wallet, don't take them out with you – even better, cut some of them up and rationalise the spending tools you have at your disposal. Your bank balance will thank you.

BEING PREPARED FOR THE WORST ISN'T ALL BAD

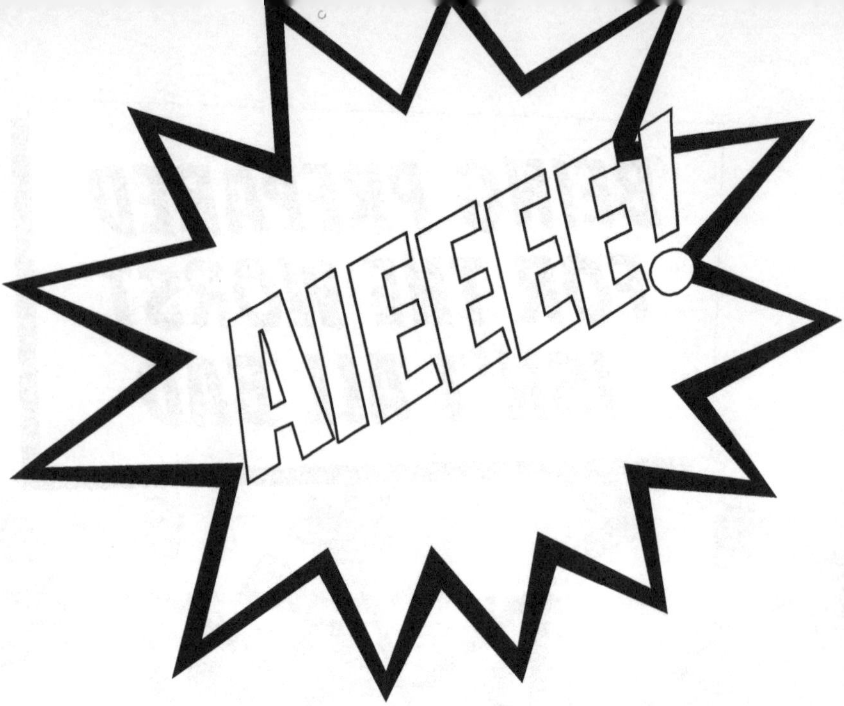
AIEEEEE!

In *The House at Pooh Corner* by A. A. Milne, Eeyore is the depressed donkey with a range of deadpan one-liners. We're particularly fond of this one:

> "People who don't think probably don't have brains; rather, they have grey fluff that's blown into their heads by mistake."

Eeyore is quite prepared for people to make silly decisions and whenever those he meets make him promises he takes those promises with a pinch of salt. We don't think that's a bad approach at all.

Right at the beginning we spoke about how we so often want to believe that people have our best interests at heart and how much easier it is just to assume what we're told is the truth.

Well, take a look at the news. Bad decisions are costing the man and woman in the street a fortune – starting from supermarket multi-buys that cost more than single items all the way up to buying insurance we'll never be eligible to claim on. Sometimes we're all guilty of having grey fluff where our brains should be.

So, starting today, assume the worst. Ask all those gloomy 'what if' questions:

1. What if I lose my job?
2. What if my marriage ends?
3. What if that person in the smart suit just wants their commission and doesn't care a hoot if this product or service is right for me?
4. Why should anyone but me have my best interests at heart?

On the surface, this may seem like a terrible gloomy way to live but it isn't. Look for the worst case scenario, plan for it or avoid it, and it's surprising how wonderful life can be. Money Fight Club members don't stand out in a crowd because they're scowling and fearful but because they're confident and assertive. They know bad things happen and they're prepared. They get into fewer financial scrapes, with the result that they are economically fit and healthy.

If your bank balance is in the black and you know you can pay your bills, life's ups and downs don't tend to trip you up so badly. Looking at the downside isn't gloomy – it's empowering. The real donkeys are the ones who automatically assume bad things won't happen. As a Money Fighter, you always ask *what if?*

Running worst-case scenarios in your head right from the start means you're less likely to panic if things do start to go wrong. One thing that often compounds a poor purchase is a panic sale. If you've considered what can go wrong, you may have avoided a mistake altogether, or at least have some idea what needs to be done when things start to unravel. You're also more open to spotting the early warning signs.

Ultimately, it's about placing your trust and confidence in the one person you should trust and feel confident about – you.

Now, get out there and kick some butt!

APPENDICES

APPENDICES

SAVING!

SAMPLE EMAIL

From: your email address

To: the person you want to respond to your complaint

Cc: other email recipients – perhaps CEO, or someone more senior at the same company

Subject: say something very simple (aim for five words or less) – such as: Complaint about ... Action required.

Unlike a traditional letter, don't put the postal address or your address at the top of the email body text itself, or bother with the date.

Dear [name],

Explain why you're getting in contact. Write a very short, unemotional description of what happened and why you're complaining. Including relevant dates and what you have done so far – complained in store, spoken on the phone, etc.

Outline, simply, what you want them to do – refund, replacement, discount...

Specify when you want them to do it by or the date by which you expect a response.

Ask them to acknowledge receipt of your email as soon as they get it.

Put your name, postal address and phone number/s at the bottom.

SAMPLE LETTER

> Your address Line 1
> Your address Line 2
> Town/County
> Postcode
> Telephone number
> Email address
>
> Their address Line 1
> Their address Line 2
> Town/County
> Postcode
>
> Date
>
> **For the attention of:** [the name and title of the main person you're writing to]
>
> **Copied to:** [names and titles of the other people you're bringing your complaint to the attention of]
>
> *Unlike an email you will have to print off and post copies of the letter to each person named. Check if they work at the same or different addresses. Never put them all in one envelope to save stamps!*
>
> <u>*Add a clear title that briefly covers what you're writing about just here (and underline it).*</u>
>
> Dear [name],
>
> *Explain why you're getting in contact. Brief details.*
>
> *What you want them to do.*
>
> *When you want them to do it by or the date by which you expect a response.*
>
> Yours sincerely,
>
> *Sign your letter here*
>
> *Print your name underneath your signature.*

DIRECTORY

Here is our quick guide to legislation, regulators, small claims court and comparison websites.

LEGISLATION

SALE OF GOODS ACT

Under the Sale of Goods Act and its various additions the things we buy have to be as described, fit for purpose and of satisfactory quality. This applies to shops and online retailers. Too often shops try to escape their responsibility and suggest customers should contact the manufacturer. This is wrong. The complaint is with the person who sells the goods, not the manufacturer.

- You should get a refund if faulty, incorrectly described or not fit for purpose.
- You don't need a receipt but may need proof of purchase.
- If the item was bought in a sale and a fault or defect was indicated, your rights would be limited but you could still complain. For example, if your fridge was cheaper because it was ex-display and scuffed it should still work properly!

TRADE DESCRIPTIONS ACT

It's a criminal offence to make false statements to achieve a sale. The local Trading Standards Department will want to hear from you if information about the materials an item is made from, its qualities, claims that it's cheaper or better than another product of the same type, etc., are untrue.

You can find your local Trading Standards' location here: www.tradingstandards.gov.uk/advice

SUPPLY OF GOODS AND SERVICES ACT

If you have problems with builders or other tradesmen you may be able to get redress under the Supply of Goods and Services Act. Goods supplied must be of satisfactory quality, services must be carried out with care and skill, within a reasonable time and for a reasonable price. The price should be fixed in advance and should not change unless you change the specification of the work being carried out.

If you have a problem with the work complain to the company supplying the services and if they are part of a bigger company complain to the head office. Many are members of trade associations that may have a mediation service, but you don't have to accept their recommendation, especially if you think they are backing a member who is in the wrong. Once again the Citizens Advice Bureau can help if you want to take your case to the Small Claims Court.

You should be able to get a local solicitor to send a letter setting out your claim and this should pay for itself if it gets the company to respond more quickly.

CONSUMER CREDIT ACT

Nowadays most of us pay for expensive items with a loan or credit card. This can provide extra protection if things go wrong.

Under Section 75 of the Consumer Credit Act you can also claim against the credit card company if the retailer or builder won't entertain your claim, or has gone bust. This protection is available on items costing from £100 to £30,000. You can find details of how to claim online at your credit card company's website.

If the terms of any credit deal are unfair the Office of Fair Trading (OFT) **www.oft.gov.uk/consumer-advice**, which oversees all consumer credit licences, should be able to help you. Just being expensive is unlikely to be enough to get a deal changed.

The Financial Conduct Authority takes over from the OFT in April 2014. They can be contacted at: **consumer.queries@fca.org.uk** or 0800 111 6768.

The Finance and Leasing Association (**www.fla.org.uk**) has an arbitration scheme and may also be able to help.

DISTANCE SELLING REGULATIONS

Customers of internet retailers have additional protection. They can cancel the sale up to seven working days after receiving the item, or when the service begins, without giving a reason.

Most firms ask for a reason and it's a courtesy to tell them if the item isn't as expected or is a poor fit, but you don't have to.

You should receive a full refund including delivery costs. Some websites have tried to insist that any returned items are in their original packaging and that it has not been opened. This isn't reasonable, but you should send all parts of the packaging back if you can.

DATA PROTECTION ACT

The Data Protection Act protects us from the abuse of any data held by financial, medical, and government departments and other organisations. The Information Commissioner makes sure data isn't abused. Its free helpline is free on 0303 123 1113.

SCHEMES AND REGULATORS
FINANCIAL SERVICES

While it's often easy to see if a pair of shoes isn't fit for purpose, or that a washing machine is faulty, bank customers and investors may not know for years if they've been mis-sold a product or service or misled in some other way.

The Financial Conduct Authority regulates the financial services industry in the UK. This covers mortgages, banking, investments and insurance. The Authority does not investigate individual complaints but the firms they regulate must have a procedure in place for resolving disputes. (**www.fca.org.uk**) and consumer helpline 0800 111 6768.

FINANCIAL OMBUDSMAN SERVICE (FOS)

The FOS helps investment and banking customers who have a complaint about a company. The ombudsman also covers mortgages. It costs nothing for the consumer to make a complaint, but the banks, insurance companies and other investment organisations pay £500 for complaints that have to be mediated.

The FOS can be contacted on 0800 023 4567, which is free from landlines. You can also contact the Ombudsman at **complaint.info@financial-ombudsman.org.uk**. The postal address is The Financial Ombudsman Service, South Quay Plaza, 183 Marsh Wall, London E14 9SR.

PENSIONS OMBUDSMAN

This service investigates complaints about how pension schemes are run. It's free and can be contacted at **enquiries@pensions-ombudsman.org.uk** or 020 7630 2200. Its postal address is Office of the Pensions Ombudsman, 11 Belgrave Road, London SW1V 1RB.

PENSIONS ADVISORY SERVICE

This is an independent non-profit organisation that offers free information on company, stakeholder and personal pensions. Their website is **www.pensionsadvisoryservice.org.uk**. You can write to them at The Pensions Advisory Service, 11 Belgrave Road, London SW1V 1RB, or call 0845 601 2923.

OFGEM

Energy complaints are handled by the Energy Ombudsman who can be contacted on 0330 440 1624 or by post at Ombudsman Services: Energy, PO Box 966, Warrington, WA4 9DF. Ofgem is the regulator of Energy companies. In England contact 020 7901 7295 or online at **consumeraffairs@ofgem.gov.uk**. In Scotland contact 0141 331 2678 and in Wales contact 029 2044 4042.

OFWAT

Water companies are regulated by Ofwat, who will deal with complaints. They can be contacted on 0121 644 7500 or at **mailbox@ofwat.gsi.gov.uk**.

CONSUMER COUNCIL FOR WATER

This organisation will help you if Ofwat does not resolve your complaint. It's on 0121 345 1000 and online at **enquiries@ccwater.org.uk**.

OFCOM

Problems with telecoms companies, postal deliveries and television, radio and satellite companies should be directed to Ofcom (**www.ofcom.org.uk**). It's based at Riverside House, 2a Southwark Bridge Road, London SE1 9HA. Telephone 0300 123 3333 or 020 7981 3040.

OMBUDSMAN SERVICES

For more information about Ombudsman Services, you can get in contact by emailing **enquiries@ombudsman-services.org**.

These services also cover complaints involving letting agents and the Green Deal scheme. Its postal address is Ombudsman Services, The Brew House, Wilderspool Park, Greenall's Avenue, Warrington, WA4 6HL.

COURT

SMALL CLAIMS COURT

Before making a claim in the courts you need to give the offending organisation a chance to put things right. So, for example, complain in person at the shop where the item was bought or by email/phone to an internet trader.

Follow up by letter to head office and if you get nowhere consider taking your complaint to your local authority Trading Standards Department or talking to your local Citizens Advice Bureau (CAB). You can also find really useful CAB advice online (**www.adviceguide.org.uk/england**).

Before you can make a claim you have to send a final warning letter and it's surprising how this can encourage a retailer to see sense.

Claims are limited to £5000. The fees start at £35 for a claim up to £300 and they rise to £120 for up to £5000.

Most claims involve faulty items that cause the retailer as much grief as the customer but occasionally a shop or website will try to mislead customers into buying something. When this happens there's further protection available.

Claim forms are available from local courts and from HM Courts and Tribunals Service at **www.hmcourts-service.gov.uk**.

YOUR RIGHTS AND THE LAW

A good starting point for clarifying your rights is the Justice section of the Gov.uk website: **www.gov.uk/browse/justice/rights**

PRICE COMPARISON WEBSITES
ENERGY BILLS
www.ukpower.co.uk
www.theenergyshop.com/HomeEnergy
www.unravelit.com
energylinx.co.uk
www.fuelswitch.com
www.which.co.uk/switch
www.energyhelpline.com

ALL PRODUCTS
www.uswitch.com
www.simplyswitch.com
www.moneysupermarket.com
www.moneyfacts.co.uk
www.confused.com
www.moneysavingexpert.com
www.moneyhelpline.com
www.telecomshelpline.com/broadband

MOBILE PHONES
www.billmonitor.com

INSURANCE
www.gocompare.com
www.confused.com
www.comparethemarket.com

GOODS

www.pricerunner.co.uk
www.ciao.co.uk
www.kelkoo.co.uk
www.shopping.com

TRAVEL

www.travelsupermarket.com
www.trivago.co.uk
www.skyscanner.net
www.kayak.co.uk

INDEX

INDEX

99p Stores 54
08** numbers 86, 88, 90,
18185.co.uk 90

advertising (misleading) 25, 53, 55, 75, 112, 140, 153, 158
air travel 154-7
Ali, Muhammad 1, 15
asking questions 25-6, 31, 184, 219
Association of Residential Letting Agents (ARLA) 140

Balboa, Rocky 45
bank base rate
banks/building societies 7-8, 19-20, 86, 101-15, 120, 190
  mergers 109
Bank of Ireland 130
Barclays 12
bicycles 168-9
Bill Monitor (www.billmonitor.com) 91, 251
bills see household bills
body language 35
Bonaparte, Napoleon 172
brand loyalty 61-2
British Gas 12
British Insurance Brokers' Association (www.biba.org.uk) 170
British Telecom (BT) 84
broadband 70, 84, 85, 92-4, 139
budgeting 124-5, 139, 189, 211-6
bundles 70, 85, 93
bus travel 152, 158, 166-7

call centres 20, 26, 33, 37-8
calm (importance of staying) 25, 29, 33, 34, 44, 133
cancellation charges 85, 93-4
capital gains tax 203-4
cars *see also* motoring

buying a new car 159
buying a second hand car 160-1
car clubs 168
hiring 167-8
cash (use of) 215-6
cash-back 73, 75, 105, 106
  cards 60
cash machine(s) 104, 107
Centre for Economics and Business Research 64
claims managers 42-3 *see also* no-win, no-fee
cold calling 16, 17, 26, 43
complaining 27, 29, 33-8, 41, 43-4, 64, 101, 106, 172, 225, 226, 228, 229, 230
  ACT 44
  by email 39
    sample 223
  by letter 39-40
    sample 224
  by phone 36-8
  in person 33-5
  structure of 46
commuting 150-2, 166, 168-9, 188, 189
conformism 15-16
confusion marketing 13
congestion charge (London) 150, 158
cons 1, 7, 11-12, 52, 56, 57, 69, 101 see also scandals
Consumer Council for Water (CCW) 81, 229
Consumer Credit Act 156, 226-7
contactless cards 102, 214-5
Cost of a Child report 178
council tax 77-81
  bands 78
  discounts and waivers 80-1
  valuation process 77-9
Cox, Nigel 40
credit and debit cards 60, 94, 102,

109-111, 125, 127, 156, 210, 215
  fees when paying with 110, 156
  travel insurance 170
  use of abroad 104-5, 106, 111, 157
credit checks 126-7
credit unions 114-5
current accounts 103-7
  interest 105
  monthly, and other, fees 105-6
  switching 103-4
Cycle to Work Alliance (www.cycletoworkalliance.org.uk) 169

Data Protection Act 227
death 157, 193-4, 204-5
debit cards see credit and debit cards
deposit protection schemes 141
deregulation 8-10
distance selling regulations 40, 227
divorce 23, 177, 190-2, 193

electrical appliances 73-4, 77, 83, 123
electricity 70-1, 74, 76, 96, 139, 210, 214
email addresses, typical format of 39
embarrassment 15, 20-1, 23, 58, 59
Energy Bill 71
energy bills 52, 69, 75, 251
  checking recent 71-2
  direct debit payment 72
  dual fuel 71
  incorrect 73
  insurance/warranties 77
  overpayment 72
  switching supplier 76
  tariffs 75
energy usage patterns 75
energy saving tips 74
estate agents 119, 120, 133, 134-5, 140, 144

European Health Insurance Card (EHIC) 169
excess (insurance) 88, 95, 163, 164, 170, 171

Fiennes, Ranulph 69
fighting styles 33-44
Finance and Leasing Association (www.fla.org.uk) 227
Financial Conduct Authority (FCA, www.fca.org.uk) 11, 12, 88, 102, 108, 227, 228
financial fitness test 31-2
Financial Ombudsman Scheme (FOS, www.financialombudsman.org.uk) 101, 132, 228
flood risk 95, 136
food shopping
  check ingredients 62-3
  difficulty of comparing prices 54-5, 57, 61-3
  local markets 54, 57
  online 63-4
  packaging 51, 55-6
  tactics 55
  where to find the best bargains 52-3
Frazier, Joe 15
free gift 22, 25
FTSE 100 180

gas 71, 72, 69-71, 74, 76, 96, 125, 139, 210, 213-4
golden rules of Money Fight Club 29-30

Helmsley, Leona 199
Her Majesty's Revenue and Customs (HMRC) 199-201, 203
  difficulty contacting 203
Herman, Richard 16, 43
horse meat scandal 12, 52
household insurance 94-5, 143
  flood risk 95, 136

illness 192-3
income tax 201-3
   rates 201-2
inheritance tax 204-5
interest rates
   paying 11, 104, 109-11, 111-12, 123, 128, 152, 199, 209, 210
   receiving 25, 105-6, 108-9, 179, 201-2, 209
   taking a view on future rates 128-9
international phone calls 84, 85, 89-90, 91
investing 180-2, 195
   in forestry 204
   shares 179-81
ISA (Individual Savings Account) 108

Jobseeker's Allowance 189

Kent, John 201

Land Registry (www.landregistry.gov.uk) 134, 135
Laozi 149
lawyers see legal advice
laziness 19, 21, 32
legal advice 188, 191
Lewis, Lennox 25
Libel 44
Libor 12, 103
Lloyds 19
loans 111-115, *see also* payday loans

Macmillan Cancer Support 193
manners 27, 33-4, 43-4, 45
Medical Travel Compared (www.medicaltravelcompared.co.uk) 170
Megabus (www.megabus.com) 167
meter
   pre-payment 73, 76
   readings 72, 74, 76
   water 81-3
mobile phones 86-92
   insurance 88-9
Money Facts (www.moneyfacts.co.uk) 105, 234
Money Fight Club (www.moneyfightclub.com) 5, 31, 39, 40, 45, 75, 85
   fitness test 31-2
   golden rules 29-30
   money fighter attributes 25-7
Money Saving Expert (www.moneysavingexpert.com) 143, 251
www.moneysupermarket.com 143, 231
mortgages 124-32
   being attractive to lenders 124
   brokers 133
   credit record 126-7
   fixed vs. variable rates 128-9
   flexible vs. offset 130-1
   interest only 131-2
   produce a budget 124-5
   trackers 130
   work out what you can borrow 127
motoring 22, 157-9
   breakdown cover 166
   buying a new car 159
   buying a second hand car 160-1
   hiring a vehicle 167-8
   car clubs 168
   insurance 163-5
      making a claim 163-5
   petrol 162
Mulgrew, Gary 7
multi-buys 6, 53-4, 57, 60-1, 65, 219
   see also supermarket(s)

National Association of Estate Agents

(NAEA) 140
National Employment Savings Trust (NEST) 183-4
National Insurance 125, 184-5, 201-3, 210
National Savings & Investments (NSI) 19
NatWest 86
Netflix (www.netflix.com) 92
nice (overly) 19-20
no win-no fee 26, 42-3, 46

Ofcom 36, 88, 94, 229
Ofgem (www.ofgem.gov.uk) 11, 70, 229
Office of Fair Trading (OFT) 11, 113, 149, 226
Office for National Statistics (ONS) 52, 157
Ofwat 83, 229
ombudsman services 36, 40, 101, 132, 228, 229
online banking 106
overdraft 102, 104, 108
 charges 209, 210, 212

payday loans 11, 112-4
payment protection insurance (PPI) 20, 42, 101, 190
pensions 182-7
 advisory service (pensionsadvisoryservice.org.uk) 228
 annuities 186-7
 Department of Work and Pensions (www.dwp.gov.uk) 186
 getting the maximum when you retire 186-7
 keeping track 185-6
 moving jobs 185-6
 ombudsman 228
 personal 184
 rule of thumb guide to what you need saved 183
 state 184-5
  calculator 186
 workplace 183-4
phones 84-92
 landline 84-6
  saving money 85
 mobile 86-90
  contracts 87-8
  fashion 86
  insurance 88-9
  international calls 89-90
  sim-only deal 81
 money saving tips 91-2
Poundland 54
Powell, Colin 177
power of attorney 193
planning for stages of life 177-9
Premium Bonds 19
premium rate phone numbers 36, 84, 86, 164, 203
price comparison websites 64, 75, 91, 151, 160, 231-2
privatisation 71, 81
property
 buying and selling 120-38
  emotions 132, 133, 135, 144-5
  estate agents 119, 120, 133, 134-5, 140, 144
  mortgages 119-20, 124-32
   being attractive to lenders 124
   brokers 133
   costs and problems
   credit record 126-7
   downsizing 138
   fixed vs. variable rates 128-9
   flexible vs. offset 130-1
   interest only 131-2
   produce a budget 124-5
   retirement property 137-8

INDEX

stamp duty 135-6
trackers 130
work out what you can borrow 127
new builds 123-124
ownership incentives 121-3
valuers/surveyors 134
council tax 77-81
bands 78
discounts and waivers 80-1
valuation process 77-9
renting 119-20, 138-2
agents and landlords 140
relationship with 140
contract 141-2
deposit 141
what you can afford 139

Railcards 150, 151
Rambo 8, 9, 12
Rebtel (www.rebtel.com) 89-90
receipts 31, 52, 54, 61
redundancy 188-9
renting 119-20, 138-2
agents and landlords 140
relationship with 140
contract 141-2
deposit 141
what you can afford 139
retirement planning 178 *see also* pensions
Review Centre (www.reviewcentre.com) 41
rightmove (www.rightmove.co.uk) 134
rights 29, 45-6, 230
Royal Institute of Chartered Surveyors (RICS) 119

Sale of Goods Act 225
sales techniques 20-1

saving 111, 116, 179-82, 190, 195
savings accounts 108-9, 201-2
SayNoTo0870.com 86
scandals cons 1, 7, 11-12, 52, 56, 57, 69, 101 *see also* scandals
shares 179-81
share scheme 179-80
sim-only deal 81
Skype (www.skype.com) 84, 90
slander 44
small claims court 46, 226, 230
Smallman, Daphne 53
small print 25, 31, 86, 88, 90, 91, 130, 143, 155, 168
social housing 142-3
social media 26, 41-2
social norms 22-3
social status 16, 144
South Sea Bubble 11, 209
supermarket(s) 23, 27, 29, 51-2, 53-8, 61-2, 76, 112, 162
competition
end-of-aisle displays 55
horse meat scandal 12, 22, 52
multi-buys 6, 53-4, 57, 60-1, 65, 219 *see also* supermarket(s)
offers and promotions 15, 61-3, 64, 65, 209, 219
vouchers 56, 58-60
Supply of Goods and Services Act 226
Swinson, Jo 56

tax 199-206
capital gains tax (CGT) 203-4
codes 200
income tax 180, 201-3
rates 201-2
over and underpayment 199-200
P60 203
personal allowance 201
television 92-94

239

contracts 92, 93-4
  HD Freeview 93
  YouView 93
Tesco 53, 58, 63
Thatcher, Margaret 9
Trade Descriptions Act 225
train travel 150, 151-2, 153-4
  advance fares 153
travel 149-173 *see also* air travel, motoring, train travel
  cost of 149
  insurance 169-71
  to work 150-2
Trip Advisor (www.tripadvisor.com) 41
trust 12, 20, 23, 25, 32, 52, 60

unit pricing 61-3
user groups (offline) 42
user review websites 41
uSwitch (www.uswitch.com) 72, 85, 251
utility companies 8, 15, 71, 75, 76, 77, 86, 90, 96, 195

VAT 21
voice over internet (VOIP) 84, 90
vouchers 56, 58-60

watchdog 1, 69
water supply 81-3, 96, 125, 159, 210, 229
  meters 81-3
  reducing consumption 81-2
weddings, cost of 178, 187
Wenban, Judith 59
Which? 11, 69, 84, 88, 90, 95, 104, 126

Zoopla (www.zoopla.co.uk) 134, 135